THE MAN WHO LOVED GEORGIA TECH

A STORY OF THE REMARKABLE LIFE OF THE HONORABLE LAWRENCE WOOD "CHIP" ROBERT, JR.

THE MAN WHO LOVED
GEORGIA TECH

A STORY OF THE REMARKABLE LIFE OF THE HONORABLE LAWRENCE WOOD "CHIP" ROBERT, JR.

1887-1976

For Nancy,
Susan S. Robert

SUSAN S. ROBERT

Copyright © 2017 by Susan S. Robert.

All rights reserved, including the right of reproduction
in whole or in part in any form.

Printed in the U.S.A. by
Gorham Printing, Centralia, Washington

ISBN 978-0-692-92200-2

*For all the support he has given,
and all the patience he has shown,
I dedicate this book to the love of my life,
my husband, Chip.*

CONTENTS

1. Preface xi
2. Introduction xiii
3. Every Life has a Beginning—The Early Years 1
4. The Georgia Tech Years 7
5. Into the World of Business—Robert and Company Begins 17
6. Chip in Washington Part I—Roosevelt's Right-Hand Man 29
7. Evie 43
8. Chip in Washington Part II—Into World War II 55
9. A Time For War—All Hands on Deck 65
10. Post-War Europe: The Marshall Plan and More Than Half a Million Miles 81
11. Circling Back Home 93
12. Every Life has an Ending 105
13. Acknowledgements 112
14. Sources Consulted 115

Invictus

Out of the night that covers me,
Black as the Pit from pole to pole,
I thank whatever gods may be
For my unconquerable soul.

In the fell clutch of circumstance
I have not winced nor cried aloud.
Under the bludgeonings of chance
My head is bloody, but unbowed.

Beyond this place of wrath and tears
Looms but the horror of the shade,
And yet the menace of the years
Finds, and shall find me, unafraid.

It matters not how straight the gate,
How charged with punishments the scroll,
I am the master of my fate:
I am the captain of my soul.

William Ernest Henley

PREFACE

NEVER HAVING WRITTEN a book before, I first turned to the dictionary definition of 'Preface' and found the following two meanings:

> The introduction of the cannon of the mass ending with the sanctus and,
> An introduction to a book telling its purpose or plan.

This book had its true beginnings at Monticello, Georgia, in 1887, when Lawrence Wood "Chip" Robert, Jr. was born. The story of this book comes to an end on June 9, 1976, the day when Chip passed away in Atlanta, at Emory University Hospital. He was 88 years old when he died, but the legacy of Lawrence Wood "Chip" Robert. Jr. will live on through his good deeds and his noble character.

Before he died, Chip gave his professional and personal papers to his daughter Birney Robert. These papers consisted of every letter he had ever sent or received, plus other papers and documents. Chip had preserved a complete and original record of his entire, very active, life.

Since his death, his daughter Birney warehoused this collection of files, boxes, suitcases, crates, trunks, and other containers in various buildings at her home in Virginia. The entire collection of materials has remained unopened for more than forty years.

A few years ago Birney moved to North Carolina and brought all the papers still unopened, along with her. At some point after hearing Birney and my husband Chip (Lawrence Wood Robert, IV) tell many astonishing and remarkable stories surrounding the life of her father (my husband's grandfather) I became curious about the contents of his papers. Soon we began to examine the containers and I began taking notes. After about a year it became clear that I had enough notes, not only for an outline, but for a family remembrance of Chip's life.

Although I had never met this man, I came to know him through his own written words, public records of his accomplishments and biographical notations which had been written about him for interviews, mostly in connection with newspaper articles and formal tributes. I was swept away by his personality and patriotism. I came to believe that his story was one of the most compelling I had ever known. As I made outlines about his life it seemed possible that I might have enough information to write such a story about Chip Robert's life.

This story does not pretend to be a biography, nor does it qualify as an historical volume. My plan for this book was to paint a picture in words about the character and temperament of Chip Robert, Jr. and of his professional and personal accomplishments. It is a great adventure story, a fairytale romance and a thrilling international war saga. It is a survey of his life painted in broad brush strokes, really just a thumbnail sketch.

I am happy to leave to others the privilege of writing a proper biography. I have not the skills to set upon such a complicated task, but I hope that many will come to explore, study and research his papers where they will be archived at the Rose Library. For the first time it will be possible to learn of all the fascinating stories that made up the life of Lawrence Wood "Chip" Robert, Jr.

Fortunately, the Stuart A. Rose Manuscript, Archives, and Rare Books Library at Emory University has acquired the entire collection of Chip Robert's papers and other materials. This 88-year record of the life and times of Chip Robert and his multiple public and private careers will be available for scholars, researchers, professors and students to examine and explore. This gift has been made in the hope that the record of his life will be of profound interest and value to future generations seeking to understand our past to better prepare for the future.

Susan S. Robert
June 18, 2017
Highlands, NC

INTRODUCTION

EVERY LIFE HAS a beginning and every life has an ending, and somewhere in between, every life tells a story. Some lives tell more than one story. But every now and then, a person appears whose narrative is so compelling and filled with such action and adventure that, although their time on the Earth has ended, the story of their life continues to resonate long after they have gone.

Such is the story of the remarkable life of The Honorable Lawrence Wood "Chip" Robert Jr., whose entire life was nothing short of 'a work of art.'

"Chip," as he shall be named during the course of this book, was born September 3, 1887, and he died on June 9, 1976. In between, his life straddled two centuries and he lived a dozen stories. He was a man in full.

This is a book about a man who seemed larger than life. He was a hero in his own time, and he left behind countless legacies of accomplishments in both his professional and personal life. He lived by a set of values and high ethical standards, values just as relevant in the present as they were in the past—loyalty, generosity, gratitude and sacrifice—these were ever present in his character.

After sailing his way through Georgia Tech, setting records which were still unbroken when he died, Chip began his professional career as an engineer, and by the mid-twenties, he had become an industrial tycoon.

By 1917, he had founded a firm, "Robert and Company" destined to become one of the largest and most prominent architectural and engineering companies in the world.

During Chip's long and successful career, he was called by many titles, some more formal than others. He was called the 'best deal maker in the nation', and 'Roosevelt's righthand man'. He was a member of Roosevelt's inner circle, and was called 'the glamour boy of Washington', 'the force behind the National Recovery Act,' and 'a leading architect of the PWA.' He was The Honorable Assistant Secretary of the Treasury, The Honorable Secretary of the Democratic National Committee, and the founder and Executive Director of the Southern Governors' Conference.

He was also a confidant of President Truman, and one of the lead delegates in charge of the reconstruction of Europe, called the Marshall Plan.

He was among the leading experts on international affairs, having traveled the world since the 1920's, and after 1947, having made 17 complete trips around the globe, probably a long distance record for any private citizen.

And probably the title he wore with the greatest pride was that of "Mr. Georgia Tech." For more than seven decades, he was beloved by students, faculty and alumni of Tech all over the world.

And so, here begins a story of a patriot and a citizen who served his Country and especially his beloved South. It is the story of Lawrence Wood Robert, Jr., The Man Who Loved Georgia Tech.

CHAPTER ONE

Every Life has a Beginning– The Early Years

Travel is fatal to prejudice, bigotry and narrow mindedness, and many of our own people need it solely on these accounts. Broad, wholesome, charitable views of men and things cannot be acquired by vegetating in one little corner of the Earth all one's lifetime.

Mark Twain

Lawrence Wood "Chip" Robert, Jr., was born on September 3, 1887 in Monticello, Georgia. This small town lies 65 miles southeast of Atlanta, and is the seat of Jasper County. Monticello was named in honor of Thomas Jefferson's country estate in Virginia. The old county courthouse sits atop one of the rolling hills in the town and it remains beautiful to this day.

Typical of most Southern areas in the mid-1800's, Monticello was in an agrarian district largely farmed in cotton crops. In 1793, Eli Whitney had invented the cotton gin and made the separation of the seeds from the cotton fiber much more efficient. Between 1800 and 1950, over two million acres of cotton were planted in Georgia. By the year 1910 the population of Jasper County was 16,500 and during this era throughout the state of Georgia and all across the South, Cotton was King.

During these years, the railroads were building new lines crisscrossing the south, largely in order to ship the ever increasing cotton crops to the North to be manufactured into many different products.

Basically, all the cotton was grown and harvested by the laborers in the South, and then baled and shipped to the Northeast to the big manufacturing plants of the textile industries. This same cotton was then made into various finished products which were subsequently sent back into the South for consumption.

Chip's father, Lawrence Wood Robert, Sr. was born in Marietta, Georgia in 1859 and was known as the "Captain." He was educated at Yale, and was to become one of the South's great railroad engineers and builders.

Chip's boyhood home in Monticello, GA

Captain Robert first worked with the Georgia Pacific Railroad (then Southern Railway) running between Atlanta and Birmingham. At this time, Birmingham was still a small village and the Captain was building railroad lines in the coal and iron fields of Alabama. After a period in this district, he returned to Georgia to build numerous short line rails. His company eventually became the Central of Georgia Railroad and he began building new lines all across Georgia.

While building a line between Macon and Athens during the 1880's, Captain Robert was working around Georgia and met a beautiful young girl from an old Monticello family. He courted Miss Minnie Newton, and they married when she reached the age of eighteen. They made their home in Minnie's grandparents' house on the edge of town, and this gorgeous place still stands in Monticello today.

Minnie was busy raising their three sons, Lawrence (Chip), Pierce and Frank, with the Captain commuting to South Georgia to build railroads during the week.

Suddenly, and very tragically, Minnie became ill and died when Chip was only nine years old. Her illness may have been consumption, which her father had contracted during the Civil War, but this is not known for certain. The two younger boys went to live with Minnie's parents in Monticello, and Chip joined his father in Brunswick.

Every Life has a Beginning—The Early Years

Chip's mother, Minnie, reading a letter from Captain Robert to her sons

During Chip's early school days in Monticello, he first learned about Henry W. Grady, the great orator and editor of *The Atlanta Constitution*. who became his lifelong hero. Chip was required to memorize sections of Grady's speeches, and he studied all of his writings. He said he was especially influenced by the speech Henry Grady had made in New York City in December, 1886, titled 'The New South.' In this address, Grady spoke of the industrialization of the South, and of the South's new abilities to change and to prosper in the dawn of a new age. He believed that the South could accomplish anything, and rise to be as modern and as successful as any part of the country. Toward the end of his speech, Henry Grady waxes eloquently in the following paragraphs:

> *"The old South rested everything on slavery and agriculture, unconscious that these could neither give nor maintain healthy growth. The New South presents a perfect democracy…a social system compact and closely knitted, less splendid on the surface, but stronger at the core—a hundred farms for every plantation, fifty homes for every palace—and a diversified industry that meets the complex needs of this complex age.*
>
> *The new South is enamored of her new work. Her soul is stirred with the breath of a new life. The light of a grander day is falling fair on her face. She is thrilling with the consciousness of growing power and prosperity. As she stands upright, full-statured and equal among the people of the earth, breathing the keen air and looking out upon the expanded horizon, she understands that her emancipation came because through the inscrutable wisdom of God her honest purpose was crossed, and her brave armies were beaten."*

From then on, Chip began to realize the huge potential and possibilities for the New South… his South. He said later that his main hobby was bringing industry to the South.

During the years after his mother's death, Chip often lived in the railroad camps, alongside the construction laborers, and he learned of their struggles and aspirations. He also learned to be a topnotch card player. He played poker and gin rummy and learned all the skills of card playing. Throughout his life, he was admired and feared for his card skills, and he loved to gamble in Cuba, Monte Carlo and all over Europe.(Later, President Roosevelt became a favorite card partner of Chip's)

Working alongside his father, Chip learned to survey, and how to make complicated mathematical calculations. Together, Chip and his father traveled the length of Florida to Palm Beach and across South Georgia while laying railroad lines for the Brunswick and Birmingham Railroad. This company later became the Central of Georgia Railroad.

Chip learned to measure tram roads and he calculated measurements for sawmill projects for the timber railroads. These measurements were used by the bonding companies to compute the exact amount of funding required for the railroad developers to borrow. Only after the money was secured, could the building begin. It was a pay-as-you-go arrangement, building one segment of line at a time.

In the summer of 1903, when Chip was 15, his father sent him north, headed to preparatory school at Cornell University so he could begin to study for his college education. Young Chip set off alone, still in his childhood knee britches, on a train headed for New York.

On his way, the train stopped in Atlanta for a brief layover. Chip decided to take a look around the City, and walked over to the Georgia Tech campus to visit a friend who was a student there. He immediately liked what he saw and decided to try to enroll.

Chip entered Georgia Tech as a sub-freshman, and graduated six years later with two degrees, fifteen athletic letters, and reportedly, the highest grade point average that had ever been attained by a Tech student.

And so began Chip's love affair with his alma mater, Georgia Tech–a relationship which would last throughout his long and successful career. And when his life came to its end, the newspapers across the country would report, 'Georgia Tech has lost its greatest friend.' Chip was, in every way, "Mr. Georgia Tech."

Swann Dorm Room of Chip Robert

CHAPTER TWO

The Georgia Tech Years

Oh! If I had a daughter, sir
I'd dress her in White and Gold
And put her on the campus
To cheer the Brave and Bold.
But if I had a son, sir,
I'd tell you what he'd do,
He would yell "To hell with Georgia,"
Like his daddy used to do.
I'm a ramblin' wreck from Georgia Tech
And a hell of an engineer—
A helluva, helluva, helluva, helluva
Hell of an engineer.

Ramblin' Wreck Anthem Song

Chip at Georgia Tech

In 1881, The International Cotton Exposition had put Atlanta on the map as the headquarters of the New South Movement. More than 350,000 people attended during this 3-month exposition and it was a dazzling success. Atlanta was teeming with railroad traffic and this established web of rail lines was to become her greatest strength. A new, modern terminal would soon open in 1905.

It was during this exciting time in 1903, when Chip stepped from the northbound train in Atlanta. It must have been a thrilling moment of discovery for a young boy traveling alone. Atlanta was a city pulsating with energy and activity. During his layover, Chip explored around the train station and then began walking along

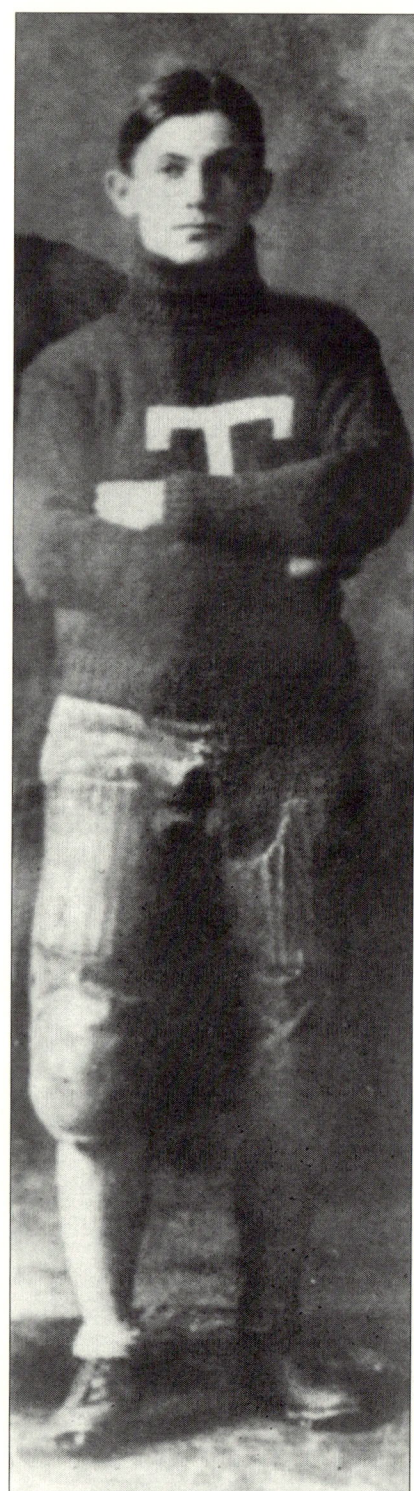

Chip, Captain of his Tech Football team, 1908

North Avenue to visit a friend who was a student at Georgia Tech. When Chip first saw the campus, he knew that this was the place for him to become an engineer. He was able to enroll for classes but the office told him that there were no rooms available. Finally, he was sent to a nearby boarding house where he could rent a room, and he soon began classes at Tech as a "sub-apprentice."

In the Fall of 1903, Georgia Tech enrolled 510 students. Mr. Lyman Hall was the President and Georgia Tech had existed for a mere sixteen years. In 1906, Dr. Kenneth Matheson would become President so Chip saw two leaderships at Tech before he graduated in 1909.

When Chip arrived at Georgia Tech, the campus was still being built. The Administration Building was constructed first in 1887, and then the Swann dormitory. In 1906, Tech was awarded a Carnegie grant for its first library.

Chip immediately immersed himself in campus life. He became a student leader and he excelled in the classroom. But, most of all, Chip loved athletics. Because he was such an excellent student, he was never required to take a final exam during his entire six years at Tech. There was a school rule that no student could play more than two sports at one time, but because of Chip's good grades, he was allowed to play without a limit. By the end of his college career, Chip had lettered fifteen times in varsity sports. He served as captain of the football team, captain of the baseball team and captain of the track team.

Chip thrived in all leadership roles. He was active in his fraternity, Sigma Nu, and served on the interfraternity council as well as the student council. He helped publish the first Tech yearbook—*The Blueprint*, and was a founder of ANAK, the senior honor society, one of the most elite groups on campus.

Chip was known far and wide for his prowess as a Georgia Tech football star. He played the position of quarterback and linebacker—offensive and defensive positions in every game. He played a full sixty minutes in every football contest and never had any time outs for injury.

Tech football squad for season 1908. Chip Robert, Captain, October 2, 1908

Tech Football, 1905

Top: **Grant Field, Georgia Tech.**
Left: **Georgia Tech athletes.**
Bottom: **Track team, 1908.**

Chip was unanimously elected for All Southern Football Honors for three consecutive years and was instrumental in changing several rules for intercollegiate football.

In 1933, a reporter asked him to describe his greatest thrill of his football career. Chip replied:

> *Oh, yes…it was that ringer game against the University of Georgia in 1908. You see, in those days, many of the colleges imported players when there was a lack of available material. Georgia was then, and always will be Georgia Tech's archrival. Georgia Tech had a good team that year and we were favored to walk all over Georgia. When the day arrived, we journeyed over to Athens, Georgia, and lo and behold! When we ran out onto that field, we saw about twenty giants on Georgia's squad! They had imported those husky fellows from up North. Most of them were great northern college players. Well, Georgia scored on us and we trailed them a touchdown behind until the last quarter. We finally managed to get to their goal, and I carried the ball over to score, 6-6. Our fullback kicked a field goal to win the game, 9-6! We were a bruised but happy bunch when we took that train back to Atlanta.*

The reporter made an observation that:

> *Robert is still very much the prototype of the ideal athlete. Though his hair is prematurely gray, he is youthful in appearance. He is yet the dynamic atom of energy that impelled him to the forefront in football. And today, the same forcefulness that carried him to the football heights is evident in the place he has attained among the Nation's Leaders.*

Football team, 1904

To help pay his way through Georgia Tech, Chip taught higher mathematics and calculus part time. He also assisted the great Coach John Heisman who was with Tech for more than 15 years.

Once Chip completed his Civil Engineering degree in 1908, his friend, Ty Cobb tried to persuade him to join with him at the Detroit Tigers Professional Baseball Team. But Chip had been given an opportunity to take an experimental engineering degree, now called Electrical Engineering, and to play on the football team for one more season. He took this opportunity and graduated with a second BS degree in 1909 as well.

Baseball banquet by Captain L.W. Robert for Southern Champions, 1906

Baseball squad, 1906

The Georgia Tech Years

Chip, Captain of his Tech baseball team, 1908

After graduation, Chip was made a member of the Alumni Board, and two years later, he was elected to the Board of Trustees where he served for twenty-four years. In 1932, Tech became a part of the Board of Regents of the University System of Georgia. After the establishment of the Board of Regents, Chip served as Chairman of the Building Committee.

Chip spent many hours on campus, tutoring the student athletes with calculus, and helping to coach the football and baseball teams, and to scout for promising high school players. He served as a member of the Georgia Tech Athletic Board for forty years.

For the remainder of his life, he was to carry Georgia Tech with him across the Nation, and throughout the World–Tech's story became a part of his story.

Georgia Tech Sigma Nu, 1908

The Georgia Tech Years

Chip's sub-apprentice class, 1903

Organization and first ANAK Society, 1908

Chip in his first office, circa 1917

CHAPTER THREE

Into the World of Business—
Robert and Company Begins

In the future days, which we seek to make secure, we look forward to a world founded upon four essential human freedoms. The first is freedom of speech and expression—everywhere in the world. The second is freedom of every person to worship God in his own way—everywhere in the world. The third is freedom from want—everywhere in the world. The fourth is freedom from fear—everywhere in the world... That is no vision for a distant millennium. It is a definite basis for a kind of world attainable in our own time.

FDR, January 6, 1941
State of the Union Address

In Atlanta, around 1910, Chip Robert was beginning his professional life. He became associated with Park Dallas, and together, they formed the firm of Dallas and Robert, Engineers. But when World War I had begun, Dallas wanted to retire and join the Army. Chip bought the firm for $250.00, and this sum included the five employees who worked at the office and all of the furnishings. Thus, Robert and Company Architects and Engineers became a business in 1917 in Atlanta, Georgia. The company was originally located in the Red Cross Building on Ivy Street, and then moved into the Candler Building in the center of town. It then relocated to the Bona Allen Building, and in 1948 settled into its own building at 96 Poplar Street.

These were difficult times for the agrarian areas in the South, and although the Great Stock Market Crash was not to happen until 1929, many Southerners were out of work. There was the 'Panic of 1907' and the ravages caused by the Boll Weevil insect which reduced the Southern cotton crops by half in 1915.

But Robert and Company was finding enough work, and the firm was busy engineering industrial buildings of all types.

Soon after graduating Georgia Tech, Chip married Miss Louise Ayers from Macon, Georgia. They had two children; a son, Lawrence Wood Robert, III born in 1912, and a daughter, Louisa Ayres Robert, born in 1914.

Chip continued to develop his business in the Southeast. Robert and Company engineered hydroelectric plants and manufacturing compounds in Georgia and Alabama and other southern states. Robert and Company was designing Coca Cola bottling plants all across the United States and engineered those facilities in Baltimore, Seattle, Boston, Los Angeles, Columbus, Chattanooga, East Hartford, Oakland and New Haven, to name a few. It was rumored that Robert and Company designed a Coca-Cola Bottling Plant in every state in the United States. The company was growing its business in the civil engineering areas and beginning to do a number of projects for the military.

In 1914, Chip was on a business trip to New York City when he learned that one of his heroes, General Leonard Wood, was serving as Army Chief of Staff at the Army-Navy Building. He was a Georgia Tech alumnus, had been the Captain of its very first football team, and went on to become a football legend around the nation. General Wood graduated from medical school and trained to be a surgeon. But eventually, he chose a career in the armed services.

Chip went to see his hero in his office, but could not get in. Finally, Chip sent word to General Wood that he had also been a football player for the Yellow Jackets and just stopped by to say 'hello.'

Chip's Coca-Cola Bottling Plant; Nairobi, Kenya

Immediately, General Wood came out to greet Chip, and they had a long visit. Then, General Wood took Chip as his guest to the Officers' Club for lunch, and they reminisced about Georgia Tech Football. Out of the blue, General Wood asked Chip to become his civilian aide for the military construction program during World War I. Chip was appointed to help him to locate the best military building sites in the United States which would be needed for the War effort.

General Wood made several visits to Georgia Tech. In 1917 he came to campus to give the commencement address for the graduating class. World War I was still going on, and this trip to Atlanta led to the connection between the Navy and the Georgia Tech Campus. The Armed Forces needed expert engineering training for its new recruits. Chip played a role in all of this.

Only six colleges in the country were chosen to establish an ROTC program which coincided with the technical training needed for the recruits to be able to operate the new ships and tanks. This was a tremendous help to Tech and the military.

So, Chip came to serve in the Army Reserves by inspecting various projects for General Wood during World War I and assisted in a civilian capacity until the end of the war on November 11, 1918. It is notable to mention that Chip never missed an Army Navy football game until the year he died.

During these early years as an alumnus of Tech, Chip was regularly volunteering and participating in school activities. He was in the group who first devised the idea of making a Tech education more accessible.

The set up was what is now known nationally the "Co-Op" program. It served as a model for a number of colleges throughout the country, and became a highly respected academic program. This cooperative program was designed whereby two students could go to school and work in a private business simultaneously and graduate in four years, practically paying for their entire education at the same time.

The pair of students was hired by one firm, each working a month in an alternating fashion, while the other attended classes at Tech. This program was continuous, twelve months a year. The students had no vacation except a week at Christmas and a week during the Summer.

As Chip reported:

This (cooperative) arrangement made it possible for boys to take a very small outlay from their parents and work their way through college and at the same time be on the job for four years with all the experience and background. The record shows that they are the most popular college men with big industry looking for ambitious high class technically educated young men. I am very proud of this Cooperative Department.

Robert and Company hired hundreds of these Co-op students throughout the years. In fact, it was often said that any engineer in Atlanta had, at one time or another, worked for Robert and Company. The co-op program existed in this format at Georgia Tech until the school

Robert and Company, circa 1920

changed from the quarter system to semesters.

Chip always said that Georgia Tech was his main interest and called the industrialization of the South his main pastime. He was fascinated by the automotive industry, and by the mid-twenties, Chip was certain that the automobile was here to stay.

Chip backed some inventions having to do with the automobile. And he owned a patent for a retractable canvas top to be used with rumble seats.

As Chip was investigating the idea of persuading the Northern manufacturers to move South he became acquainted with a certain type of cotton cording which was being produced for use in modern rubber tires. Chip observed that all of the cotton was being planted, raised, and harvested in the South, but just as it had always been, that cotton crop was baled, loaded onto trains and carried to the mills in the Northeast. As it had been for decades all the items were made in the northern factories and then back they came down to the South at a big mark up for all the southern consumers.

Chip was paying close attention to the railroad freight rates, which were markedly lower for the North than for the South and West. He first began investigating these unfair tariffs in 1915, and he was on a mission to get parity of all the shipment destinations. Chip fought constantly against this inequality arguing that these discriminatory rates gave unfair advantage to the

Northeast and kept businesses from moving their industries to the South. We note here that, regarding Federal regulatory agencies and commissions, the Interstate Commerce Commission was established in 1887, and the Sherman Antitrust Act passed in 1890.

Chip was still battling this freight rate situation in the late 1930's, but the rates did eventually become fair for all areas of the United States. In fact, this was the prime motivating force that led Chip to found The Southern Governors Conference in 1932.

But all along, Chip knew that if he could persuade the Northern industries to move South, it would mean thousands of new jobs for the area, and an overall huge boost to the textile industry for the South.

It was shortly before the time that Chip was organizing Robert and Company, that he decided to go exploring. In 1916, Chip literally disappeared for three months and headed up to the Northeast. There were three main mills which made the particular type cord which was used to make rubber tires. Production was increasing quickly because demand for the new rubber tires to use on the Army trucks and tanks.

The mills were located in Passiac NJ, Pawtucket RI, and East Hampton, Mass. Chip

Cotton Mill; NY, 1923

Viaduct Project, 1920's

managed to get jobs in each as a 'hobo twister.' As a workhand, Chip was boarded with other mill workers, most of whom were immigrant men.

After Chip's daily work shift, he lived with these workers, sharing meals and sleeping quarters and also sharing leisure time. Among these three factories, Chip learned all there was to know about cord production. Plus, he continued to improve his poker skills in the nightly card games.

When Chip returned home to Atlanta, he knew how the factories were organized and how to make the 'magic' cotton cord. Furthermore, he learned how to make the special looms and spindles which would be necessary in any mill that would be built. But his greatest discovery was to learn just how high the cost of living was in the North, as well as how brutal the cold weather could become. The cost of food, the cost of fuel, and all other costs of living required the wages to be so much higher than they would be in the South. And Chip knew that the warmer climate in the South would be enticement to most anyone.

Chip immediately set about making plans to convince the owners of the Northern factories that they would be so much better off if they would come down to Georgia, Alabama, Mississippi, and Louisiana to build their factories. He knew that none of these men had ever visited the Southern States and he had an idea.

Chip and his group of friends organized a special train tour whereby the train visited eight Georgia manufacturing towns in four days. Their guests enjoyed an abundance of Southern hospitality and delicious food. There were guided tours of big plants, and musical entertainment and even visits to formal gardens. The visitors from the North reported that they had a wonderful time and had fallen in love with the South and especially with Georgia. Two weeks later, the textile deal was announced and history was made.

On April 26, 1926, the front page banner headlines in most every major newspaper in the

Chip and friends, 1920's

country proclaimed–The Textile Deal of the Century: $100,000,000 involved in Textile Contracts Bringing Goodrich and Fisk Firms to Georgia.

The great O. B. Keeler reported for the *Atlanta Journal*, that:

> *The 'greatest deal in world history' was brought about by L.W. Robert, Jr. to make Georgia the producer of 60% of the Country's tire fabric.*

Keeler goes on to say:

> *(Georgia's) ideal climate, labor conditions, unlimited water and power, and conservative fiscal policies convinced heads of manufacturing concerns of its future greatness.*

The reporter calls Chip, the 'great textile engineer,' and says that:

> *National industry's ultimate seal of approval is set on Georgia as a cotton manufacturing state with the announcement of a contract just signed by B. F. Goodrich Company and the Fisk Rubber Company.*

Meanwhile, Chip kept in close touch with his Tech classmates. He kept watch for good high school players who they might recruit for Georgia Tech, and capitalized on the growing reputation of Coach Heisman's Golden Tornado team, who had won the National Football Championship in 1917. Then, when Coach Heisman left in 1919 after a 15-year career with Tech, assistant coach William Alexander became Tech's head coach. Unfortunately, John Heisman and his wife were getting divorced, and he gave her first choice of where she would like to live. She chose to stay in Atlanta, and Heisman accepted the head coaching job at his alma mater at Penn. He was a beloved coach and a mentor to all his players. He often said that being a good football player is not half so important as being a gentleman.

Heisman was coach in 1916 when the team made a 222 point victory over Cumberland. His coaching innovations were famous, including the quarterback safety on defense; the center tossing the ball back; a vocal signal for putting the ball in play; the double lateral pass; the spin back, and the Heisman Shift. He was instrumental in the legalization of the forward pass and for the division of the game into quarters. He was the Father of Modern Football. Heisman died in 1936. For several years Heisman had been the Director of the Downtown Athletic Club in NYC and a trophy originated by the Club the year before he died became known as The Heisman Trophy, the most coveted award in college football.

In 1921 Chip was selected to be the National Chairman of the Greater Tech Campaign. He contacted Alumni from all areas of the country, and personally called upon hundreds of 'Friends of Tech' who lived in Atlanta. He mailed a powerful letter to every alum he could locate and implored each man to step forward for their alma mater. He made the case of how valuable their Tech education was, and of the priceless gift of friendships they had all made at Tech. Chip wrote a letter to every alumnus asking each of them to contribute whatever it was in their power to give and this first capital campaign of Georgia Tech was a great success. The campaign not only met its goal but far exceeded it.

The football program at Tech was gaining huge popularity, and more and more fans were packing the stands. The number of fans had outgrown the original Grant Field and in 1924, Chip and his firm drew up all of the plans for a new stadium and gave these to Georgia Tech. The stadium was revolutionary with its U-shaped south stands, an innovation in modern design. By 1927, there were 40,000 spectators filling the stands at every home game. Georgia Tech had become a football powerhouse.

Chip had also met and become friends with Knute Rockne of Notre Dame. He began a conversation with Rockne and appeared before the Notre Dame Athletic Committee in 1921. This led to the now famous Tech-Notre Dame series, beginning in 1924. Chip and Rockne collaborated on all the agreements of time and place and how the gate revenues would be shared. They continued a lasting friendship until Rockne was killed in a plane crash March 31, 1931. Reflecting upon this collaboration, Chip had noted that football can be an instrument of goodwill and prestige, and a way for schools to learn about each other. In the beginning, football made Notre Dame and football also made Georgia Tech.

One of the great moments in Georgia Tech's history came on New Year's Eve, 1929. The University of California was playing Georgia Tech in the Rose Bowl game, and no one was surprised when Chip wanted to take a special train out to Pasadena to support the team. This train was packed with Tech fans, and the atmosphere was filled with excitement and anticipation.

Georgia Tech was victorious over the University of California, and there was much celebration. At one party, the California chapter of the Georgia Tech Alumni Assocation made Chip a gift of a young brown bear. Chip escorted the bear back on the train, where it rode to Atlanta in the mail car. When the train got back home, Chip took the bear over to Tech and gave him to Stumpy Thomason, and the bear lived in Stumpy's dorm for several years. The bear grew to weigh 300 pounds and became a favorite campus pet. The students taught the bear to drink Coca-Cola from the bottle and take a shower every day.

As the final year of the 1920's approached, America was teetering on the brink of the Great Depression and all across the Country, colleges and universities faced an uncertain future. In 1929, Georgia Tech received the most wonderful news. It was their good fortune to be awarded a Guggenheim Foundation grant of $300,000, a huge amount for those days.

Georgia Tech was becoming stronger each year, and Chip continued as one of the school's greatest champions. Chip believed that each advancement of Tech was the pride and joy of all alumni, and every student, and indeed the entire nation.

Old Seaboard Airline Railroad

The Georgia Tech T Train

Train trip, 1930's

Chip's formal portrait, Assistant Secretary of the Treasury, 1933

CHAPTER FOUR

Chip in Washington Part I–
Roosevelt's Right-Hand Man

The ebb and flow of a player's confidence is one of the strangest phenomena of competitive golf. I have discussed this angle with all the great players of my own, and later eras, and none deny or can explain the periods of uncertainty that occasionally come in the midst of the most complete assurance.

Bobby Jones

As the 1920's roared to an end, America was experiencing a downward spiral. State and local governments were stretched to the breaking point, and unemployment was rising in unprecedented proportions. Millions of people across the nation were living in poverty.

In October of 1929 the worst nightmare became reality as the United States Stock Market came crashing down. Businesses failed, banks closed their doors, and so began a three year period of misery for most everyone in America.

Men and women who were desperate for jobs could find no work at all. Entire families went to bed hungry, and most types of food were in short supply. The ruthless horror of The Great Depression had arrived with a vengeance. President Hoover was powerless to prevent the collapse of the US economy, and his efforts seemed to be too little too late.

Even though Chip could never in his life cast a Republican vote, he actually thought Hoover to be a fine man and hoped that he could succeed for the sake of the Country. Chip knew President Hoover was an honest man and he was a fellow engineer by profession. Chip volunteered in the South to help out with the President's "Share the Work Movement," and thought it to be an intelligent and popular form of relief.

Back in 1920, Chip had his first experience with politics. He was persuaded by his friends, Major John Cohen, publisher of the *Atlanta Journal*, and Clark Howell, editor of the *Atlanta Constitution*, to volunteer to work for the campaigns of Governor James Cox for U.S. President and Franklin Delano Roosevelt for Vice President. Chip's job was to raise money for these two candidates. He often said that while he really loved football and baseball, he believed that politics was the greatest game of all. From that time, until the end of his life, Chip could never let go of

Barkely holds picture of FDR at DNC, 1940

this fascination with politics, even though he never once ran for public office.

Chip accompanied a delegation to the 1924 National Democratic Convention at Madison Square Garden in NYC, where Woodrow Wilson won the nomination for President. After that, Chip attended every National Democratic Convention, as a delegate, until 1976. He was scheduled to attend the day Jimmy Carter won the nomination, which was the day Chip died. The entire convention floor went silent out of respect, and the Congressional Record published a special tribute to Chip's life of service to the Democratic Party.

Chip had also campaigned for Franklin Roosevelt in his bid for Governor of New York, and as the two men became better acquainted, Chip came to believe that Roosevelt was a rising star and was just the man the Country needed.

During these early years, Chip forged strong friendships with many of the great warhorse Democrats, such as Pat Harrison, Joe Robinson, Cordell Hull, Josephus Daniels and Max Gardner. He also made lifelong friends with Silliman Evans, Jack Garner and especially Amon Carter from Texas.

As the election of 1932 approached, Chip found that he had a grandstand seat in history. He said that when he looked back to those days he saw clearly how much he loved politics, and especially working with Democratic Chairman Jim Farley. After the 1932 Democratic Convention and a victory for FDR, Chip returned to the South to raise money. He had been a tremendous force in securing the California and Texas votes for Roosevelt and felt sure that FDR could be the next President.

After that convention, Chip said:

No bunch of Southerners ever went up the hill at Gettysburg like we fellows went up the hill at the Chicago Convention in 1932. With Jim Farley organizing the battle and with our acquaintances all over the Country; It was history in the making.

After the election, Chip never suspected that he would be asked to join Roosevelt's Administration. However, President Roosevelt and Jim Farley were successful in persuading Chip that he could be a great help to the country, due to his training as an industrial engineer. Chip already had a residence in Washington in the Mayflower Hotel, and Roosevelt stayed there for three weeks right after the election so he could have transition meetings with President Hoover.

Roosevelt invited Chip to come along with him as Assistant Secretary of the Treasury, with the responsibilities of being in charge of the Mint and all public buildings.

Chip made the decision to accept the offer to be Assistant Secretary of the Treasury, thinking that this would be a great opportunity to meet officials around Washington and Democratic leaders throughout the Nation. Most of all, Chip considered this his great chance to serve his

President Roosevelt's Little Whitehouse, Warm Springs, Georgia

Chip at his desk posing for Tech portrait painting

Country by serving this Democratic Administration.

Chip turned his leadership at Robert and Company over to his Father and other partners in the firm, and took a two-year leave of absence.

He began traveling around the Country, promoting Roosevelt's agenda for rescuing the Nation, and he realized that instead of talking cotton mills, rubber plants and iron foundries, he was promoting Franklin Delano Roosevelt. Chip said many times over the years that:

> *I have never considered myself a politician except inasmuch as politics is just as much of a business as anything else, and the rules and regulations are very similar. Salesmanship and organization are paramount.*

In Washington, the new administration's primary focus was to get America back to work. These were non-stop times for everyone working for President Roosevelt. They began their days at dawn and worked well into the night.

Chip was constantly in conferences with Jim Farley, Marvin McIntyre, Frank Walker, Ray Moley, Harlee Branch, and many other power players in the Democratic Party. They met daily with the President and made a plan to create a cabinet council. The council grew into the National Emergency Council, which embraced the President's Cabinet and ten other agency directors. Roosevelt appointed Chip to be a member of this group, and he remained a member until he resigned his position as Assistant Secretary of the Treasury.

Next, it was decided to separate the National Recovery Administration (NRA) from the Public Works Administration (PWA) and Chip was designated to organize the original structure of the PWA. Chip set up an outline for the cabinet board of public works and began the most difficult work of his public career.

Chip was also appointed in 1933 to assist Harry Hopkins with the first Civil Works Administration (CWA), because it had become apparent that the PWA was not working fast enough on its own.

When the winter of 1933 arrived, millions of Americans were still unemployed. People everywhere were looking for work and there were no jobs to be had. In the cities, soup lines stretched as far as the eye could see. It also happened that, during that same winter, on December 5, 1933, the Twenty-first Amendment was repealed, and Prohibition officially came to an end. Drinking was legal again.

Roosevelt knew that more Federal assistance was needed immediately. The administration pushed harder to set up more public construction projects and they also designed a Civilian Conservation Corps (CCC) to begin projects in the National Parks. Chip was a part of the leadership which developed the Reconstruction Finance Corporation (RFC) to help lend federal funds for construction projects throughout the Nation. The Administration also began promoting state and local infrastructure projects and government building expansion in every State.

Chip was also organizing the Public Works of Fine Arts Program, which eventually put 2,500 artists back to work. This program became a most popular and successful venture and was under the auspices of the Treasury Department. Chip was appointed head of the Advisory Committee to the Treasury on the fine arts, and Edward Bruce was the director in charge. Rather than to have the Public Art Project centralized in Washington, it was set up with 16 regional commissioners, with the idea that each commissioner should propose art projects chosen from their local territories. In Atlanta, the commissioner was Wilbur G. Kurtz.

Chip was constantly entertaining visiting dignitaries and local businessmen to introduce them to government officials. On February 20, 1934, he hosted all of the regional directors of the Public Arts Program. They were entertained at a banquet at the Mayflower Hotel, and Chip also included the directors of the leading museums in the Nation. Eleanor Roosevelt was one

Mrs. Roosevelt reviewing Public Art Project

of the original sponsors of the Arts Program.

In addition to his work on all the other relief programs, Chip headed up the Airways Department of the Public Works Program. After WWI, Chip had been a director of The Aviation Corporation, which controlled American Airlines. He was a visionary about so many things, and air travel was just one of them. Chip championed the need for more air fields and airports in the United States, and he made sure that substantial amounts of public funding went toward air transportation-related projects.

In 1934 it was Chip's honor to return to Georgia Tech to become the first recipient of Alumni Service Award. Tech had decided to start the annual tradition of honoring alumni who had achieved outstanding success in their professions and who were also marked by a devotion to their alma mater.

Below, is the citation read by Tech President M. L. Brittain on the occasion of the presentation:

Chip receiving the first Georgia Tech Alumni Service Award from President Brittain

The faculty of the Georgia School of Technology believe rather in earned rather than complimentary degrees. However, we expect to give meritorious service awards annually to the alumnus marked by eminence in his field and unusual devotion to the Institution. Therefore, today, it is my pleasant duty to present the first of these to Lawrence Wood Robert, Jr. who through the electric spark of personality is better known as 'Chip' Robert. In our opinion, he is the finest example we have of devoted service to the Georgia School of Technology. Year after year, he has expended time and effort in behalf of this institution and his love has not been lessened by reason of his work as one of the South's leading engineers or his more recent elevation to the high position of Assistant Secretary [of the Treasury] of the United States.

During the Roosevelt years, Chip had to decline many vacation invitations from friends, especially in Atlanta, where he had so many connections. He missed his trips to the Brazilian Court in Palm Beach, the Cloister at Sea Island, Cuba and New Orleans. He wrote many letters of regret in reply, often expressing a version of these sentiments:

How I do wish that I could be with you for your fine celebration. I can just close my eyes now, and remember our wonderful trips and I can picture all our happy memories and all the good times which our friendship has brought to us. Sadly, I am just now tied to the post in Washington, and can hardly see when I may ever get loose.

Senator Harry Truman at The Mayflower, 1938

One of the pleasures he missed was entertaining his friends. His loyalty to his lifelong friends was legendary, and they were constantly having fun and playing practical jokes on one another. He always found time to congratulate or sympathize with a friend, whatever the occasion, and he never forgot a birthday or anniversary. Telegrams were a favorite form of communication in those days, and he sent them often.

One celebration he refused to miss came during the Depression, when Americans looked to sports for hope. People were given hope by the great athletes of the day, and team sports were followed by all. One of these famous sports figures was the legendary Robert Tyre "Bobby" Jones, Jr., the greatest golfer in all of history. Known as "Bobby" to the world, he was loved and admired by everyone. Chip followed Bobby to as many tournaments as he could, and in 1930, Chip went to all four of the tournaments known as The Grand Slam of Golf. Chip was there for the British Amateur, the U.S. Amateur, the British Open and the U.S. Open. After Bobby won the Grand Slam, he was welcomed to NYC with a great parade. That evening, Chip and some Atlanta friends hosted a gala banquet in his honor. It was a huge dinner held at the Vanderbilt Hotel, and it was filled with Bobby's friends and admirers. The photographs depict a ballroom packed with guests dressed in formal attire. These photos are nearly thirty inches long, and still, all the guests could not be pictured at one time. A special train had been chartered from Atlanta and the party went on for days. But this was just the beginning. There were festivities honoring Bobby Jones back in Atlanta which went on for weeks.

A close friend of Chip's, the great Will Rogers, wrote in his newspaper column from Los Angeles:

Atlanta no more than gets cleaned up from one Bobby Jones celebration, until another comes along. You can easily exist in Atlanta by eating only at Jones testimonial dinners.

Chip and Will Rogers were good friends as well. They traveled together many times on the trains and planes from NY to Los Angeles, where Will Rogers was a Hollywood Star and a famous writer. Chip remembered him always pecking away at his typewriter, as Chip watched him composing his daily newspaper column as they traveled along. Chip called Will Rogers one of America's greatest citizens. He observed that while Will's column was only about twenty-five lines in length, he would write the article over and over, probably twenty-five times. Chip believed this showed extreme care and accounts for his great following.

Chip also liked to remember the times when Huey Long and Will Rogers would come to his hotel room and sit up all night talking politics. Chip always wished he had recorded those conversations because he said they were priceless. He loved to hear Will Rogers carry on about politicians, and here are a few of Chip's favorites:

The platform will always be the same.
Promise everything, deliver nothing.

One peculiar thing about a Democrat,
he would rather have applause than salary.

Democrats take the whole thing as a joke.
Republicans take it serious but run it like a joke.

No nation ever had two better friends than we have.
You know who they are? The Atlantic and Pacific Oceans.

When you get into trouble five thousand miles away from home,
you've got to have been looking for it.

Everyone in the Country was left grief stricken when Will Rogers' plane crashed in Alaska in 1935.

Chip, V.P. Garner and FDR at Jackson Day Dinner, 1933

Roosevelt and Jackson Day dinner, 1933

Robert and Company, Extension of the East Front of the Capital

Treasury officials confer with consultants on new D.C. building program

Chip and Cabinet, Washington, 1933

Chip displays first Public Art Project, 1934

Mrs. Roosevelt, Evie and James Roosevelt, 1937

CHAPTER FIVE

Evie

*We are always saying farewell to the world—always standing on the
edge of loss, attempting to retrieve some memory, some human meaning
from the silence—something which was precious and is gone.*

Adlai Stevenson

On December 21, 1972, a couple of months after Evie had passed away, a reporter wrote a sort of tribute to this remarkable woman for the *Northside Neighbor*, an Atlanta weekly newspaper:

In the busy Hartsfield Airport, nearly every weekend for the last few years, many among the hurrying throng have undoubtedly noted a man who stood out somewhat sharply from the crowd. Despite his age of past 80 years, he walked with rhythmical step down the long walkway to the plane which was to take him to Washington to be with his very sick wife....and a close observer might well have noted a facial expression indicating that, upon reaching her bedside, he would see an answer to prayers that she had become somewhat better from the severe kidney ailment that had plagued her for nearly five years.

And on Monday afternoon, week after week, the man in this sad story left a plane at the Hartsfield Airport, the airport which his firm designed and engineered in the 1950's, and walked to his waiting car. But on the return trip there was no ray of hope, just a mark of aggrieved sadness.

He was returning to his work and to his Biltmore Hotel suite with no hope that his once high spirited wife would again be with him in their home. The man, as many readers already know, was Lawrence Wood Robert...and he and his wife, Evelyn, universally known as Evie, had lived at the Biltmore and Washington's Mayflower since 1935... about half their time in each hotel.

Evelyn Walker Robert's life had its beginning on March 8, 1909 in the unlikely place of Atlanta, Georgia. Her Mother had been traveling home to Washington after a visit to Mexico, and Evie was born just a bit early in a hospital in Atlanta. No one could know then that she would eventually marry a man who called Atlanta home, and that she would make Atlanta her home too.

Evie's Father, Harold Walker was originally from Vermont. He was working in Mexico and Venezuela, developing oil fields for the Standard Oil Company of New Jersey and would become an Officer and General Counsel for that Company. Evie's Mother, Aloncita, was visiting relatives in Mexico City when she met Harold Walker and they soon were married. By the late 20s, they had made their home close to the Capitol Building in Washington, and had two children, Evie and Aldace.

Evie attended early school in Virginia, and then boarding schools in Paris. She brags that she attended five colleges but graduated from none. In 1928, she made her debut in Washington, and was then presented at the Court of St. James in London. She once told a reporter:

My Mother raised me to be a lady, but it didn't take.

Evie's grandmother was Alice McClellan Birney, who founded the National Parent Teacher Association (PTA) in 1897 along with her friend, Phoebe Apperson Hearst.

Evie spent her childhood riding horses near Warrenton, Virginia and on the Eastern Shore of Maryland at her grandmother's estate, known as "Webley." At this expansive mansion were stables where Evie kept her horses and other animals. Evie spent many of these years caring for the animals she loved so dearly.

Chip at Sea Island with daughter, Louisa, and son, Lawrence

When Evie was in her early twenties she had a brief marriage to Fielding Robinson from New York, but this ended in divorce and they had no children.

During her single years, Evie's life revolved around horseback riding. She rode in the West, as well as in the East, and she became a prizewinning equestrian in all classes of horsemanship.

Chip had been divorced from his wife, Louise, and she made her home in Atlanta where she had many friends and family. Their two children were adults by this time—their Son, Lawrence had married, and their Daughter, Louisa, had recently made her debut, and was the National Champion in

Chippie, Evie and James Cromwell, Delegate Count, 1936

backstroke swim competition. Louisa was also a member of the 1932 U.S. Olympic swim team and went to the Games in Los Angeles. She was unable to compete at the last minute because she had to be hospitalized with a sudden attack of appendicitis.

Evie first met Chip Robert at a dinner dance being held at the exclusive 1925 F Street Club in downtown Washington, DC. Chip was working in the Roosevelt Administration, and he entertained regularly at this club where politicians and business leaders gathered to socialize and network. During the 1930's, it was popular to have dances, which did not begin until around 10 p.m. and continued well into the night. Chip was a wonderful dancer and very popular with the women hoping for a dance with him. He was often mentioned in the society pages, with such quotes as;

Chip Robert was seen twirling across the dance floor with Mrs. Such and such.

These were the days in Washington when Senators and Congressmen stayed in that city most of the time. They did not go back to their districts too often, but rather gathered with friends and acquaintances in Washington, really getting to know their colleagues. Often, there were impromptu stag parties and many dinners where politicians could have private time to hash out compromise and get to know each other better outside their formal chamber offices. Chip was constantly putting politicians together in social settings. He was a master at putting deals together and getting congressmen with opposing viewpoints to come together from both sides of the aisle and work for compromise.

Once Chip had met Evie, his life was forever changed. She was widely recognized as one of the most beautiful women in Washington. Evie was tall and slender with shiny blond hair, and her eyes were pale blue. One news reporter said that her features were Grecian to perfection.

When they met, Evie was still a masterful equestrian, having ridden almost constantly since she was a child. She had horses stabled in Washington, DC, Warrenton, Virginia, and at her Grandmother's estate, Webley, on the Eastern Shore of Maryland. Evie was a frequent competitor and blue ribbon winner in shows on Long Island, at Madison Square Garden, and in the

Chip and Evie on their European Honeymoon, 1935

horse country of Virginia.

Evie and Chip courted and were married in wartime London in a civil ceremony in October, 1935. A reception followed at Claridge's, and their honeymoon in Europe was brief. She was twenty-six, and Chip was forty-eight.

Evie and Chip returned to Washington where they made their home in the Mayflower Hotel. They immediately joined the social set and began giving large dinner parties, which Evie orchestrated. They were often in New York City, where Chip had an apartment. There they hosted parties regularly at the Waldorf Astoria and Vanderbilt hotels. Often, the couple entertained at Evie's parents' home, the Villa Rosa on Massachusetts Avenue near the US Capitol.

Chip and Evie traveling, 1936

Evie was acquainted with many of the Washington elite, which included members of Congress, judges and diplomats. She was great friends with J. Edgar Hoover and a number of Generals who she had met horseback riding at Ft. Myer. Evie often rode General Patton's horses in competition.

Evie hosted countless parties for Chip, not only in Washington, New York, and Atlanta, but also in London and Paris. She was famous for her seating charts and how she arranged guests from all manner of backgrounds. She loved to integrate both political parties and different professions. She delighted in seating her guests with dinner partners they never would have expected.

Evie was famous for her stunning outfits, and sometimes her costumes were outrageous. She was known to wear her riding habit to the most elegant restaurants. Her dislike of hats was paramount.

47

Evie and Chip's parties were always the talk of Washington. By all reports, they were merry, lively and always unconventional.

In 1936, invitations were sent to announce an eighth birthday party which Evie was hosting for her favorite champion horse, John the Baptist. This might not seem remarkable, except for the fact that the party was to be at the Mayflower Hotel Lobby, which spanned an entire city block.

The floors had been covered with straw, and the dogs and horses were served hamburgers and carrots while the hotel's orchestra played Happy Birthday.

On January 30, 1939, Evie gave birth to a daughter. They named her Alice Birney Walker Robert and she has always been known as Birney. She grew up with a love of horses, dogs in particular, and all animals in general. She learned about horsemanship from her mother, and could ride almost before she could walk. For decades, Birney made her home in Warrenton, Virginia where she developed a wild life sanctuary and trained horses.

In the 1940s, Evie agreed to dress as a far eastern princess and ride atop an elephant in the circus. This was not Evie's first performance with a circus. When she was in her twenties she rode bareback dressed in a tutu, and jumped six-foot fences in Reno, Nevada. She was fearless.

She thought this was great fun and made the circus promise it would bring a mini-version of the event to a children's hospital the following day. Evie was a great philanthropist as well.

Evie riding John the Baptist, late 1930's

Birney and Evie, 1942

Chip had always loved the seashore and warm climates. In the early 1920s, he had started visiting The Cloister at Sea Island, Georgia and he was one of the first homeowners in the development. Cottage No. 12, as it was known, became the destination for countless gatherings and fun events. One regular house party was Chip and Evie's 4th of July Celebration, and the guests overflowed to the one hotel on the island, and many other cottages. Chip and Evie generously lent the cottage to employees and friends when they were not in Sea Island. In the summertime, the cottage was filled with family. There was horseback riding, fishing and oyster roasts at the end of the Island. There was golf and swimming, and at the Cloister Hotel there was dining and dancing, and weekly Bingo Nights. For most of Chip's life, Sea Island was a place of escape and relaxation. He treasured his time there with friends and family and especially with his beloved Evie.

Chip and Evie were also regular guests at the Brazilian Court in Palm Beach. During the winter season they vacationed there often each year, and often journeyed on to Cuba with groups of friends.

Annual Fourth of July Party, Sea Island, GA, 1938

There was no doubt that one of Chip and Evie's favorite travel destinations was Cuba. For Chip and his friends, who had been visiting Cuba since the early 1900's, Cuba was a place of refuge and relaxation from the hectic pace of their business lives. It was just a short trek by boat or plane from Palm Beach to the exotic island, and this vacation of fun and fishing was always a constant in Chip's schedule. Only the Revolution in 1953 would bring these trips to a halt.

In the early days Chip and Evie and their friends would travel to Cuba by boat, past the historic Morro Castle and into Havana Bay. Evie once wrote that Havana had a special smell about it—of cigars and cigarettes mixed with the smell of smoke and fish and oranges. They stayed at the National Hotel in Havana, a gorgeous building right on the ocean. The windows were completely bare to the outside and the floors were tiled throughout. One favorite meeting place was the Florida Bar, famous for its frozen daiquiris served by the famous bartender, Constantino.

Fishing was a great pastime in Cuba, and a favorite spot was Batabono on the western coast at the thinnest part of the island. Chip and Evie made the two-hour drive to arrive at the docks by 6 a.m., just before dawn. Then off they would go, out onto the sea. They fished for Tarpon and Sailfish, and many photos through the years picture Chip and Evie with their catch.

The Cuban countryside was dotted with banana and pineapple plantations, alongside great old mansions and estates. There were miniature horses roaming free, and all kinds of farm animals loose along the road. As the years rolled by they thought that this retreat would be waiting for them each season. Chip's daughter, Birney, recalls the very last visit in 1953.

Birney was traveling to Cuba with her father and a group of his friends and they had gone into the interior of the island to explore some ruins. Suddenly, one of their guides came running to their caravan shouting for them to come back to the airport and be ready to leave. Castro's army was storming Havana, and the airport would be shutting down at any moment. The party rushed back, and on the way, Chip learned of an entire school filled with American teachers, stranded with no means of escape from the island. Chip helped all of the teachers to get to the airport, and then called the Pentagon. He alerted his contacts of the emergency and asked for a plane to help them all escape. Within an hour, an Army transport plane had been dispatched to Havana. The plane was able to land, but it never turned off its engine. The entire group of American citizens were hastily loaded on board and everyone escaped unharmed. In fact, this was the last US plane out of Cuba.

Some of the couple's regular trips were to the Kentucky Derby where Chip went a total of forty-two times, and to the Metropolitan Opera during the month of May. When the Met came to Atlanta's Fox Theater, Chip and Evie hosted large late-night dinner parties after the opening nights of the Operas.

When they traveled to Churchill Downs, Chip took a private train and parked his cars by the racetrack where he always entertained his guests who came to the races with him. He had special box seats, and loved to bet on the ponies.

Chip and Evie at Palm Beach 1936

Evie continued to help her husband with his entertaining in Washington and Atlanta, especially with the many Georgia Tech parties Chip loved to host. Before every home football game Chip had large brunches to kick off the game day either at the Piedmont Driving Club or Capital City Club and Evie designed clever invitations for him. They were a team in every way.

For a decade, beginning in 1939, Evie wrote a weekly newspaper column for the old *Washington Times-Herald*. The paper was owned by one of her closest friends, Eleanor "Cissy" Patterson, and this column was called "Eve's Rib". These articles had a lot of society news, but they were also highly political. Evie was acquainted with practically every political star inside the beltway, and as a loyal Democrat, she had an informed opinion on most issues of the day.

Until she became too ill in her last years, Evie continued to host countless parties for Chip. In his absence on his many trips abroad she took care of his mail, working alongside Chip's longtime secretary Miss Evelyn Lewis at Robert and Company in Atlanta. Evie relayed to him what was important, and attended to the rest herself. She served as his confidential secretary in Washington while he was Secretary of the Democratic National Committee. Occasionally, she would stand in for Chip as greeter at the Democratic National Conventions. Evie was considered a most capable businesswoman and always aided Chip in his political and business endeavors.

A paramount feature of Evie's story is her lifelong love and devotion to animals—all animals. She fought tirelessly for animal rights, and served as a leader in many conservation projects. She was the founder of the Friends of the Atlanta Zoo, and she and Chip sponsored the adoption of many species of wild animals both for the Atlanta and Washington Zoos. More than once, she traveled to Africa in chartered planes to visit the great wildlife refuges near Nairobi, and she enjoyed being the first to ride out on horseback for the morning safaris. When she brought a pair of leopard cubs to the Zoo in Atlanta, she bottle-fed them both herself.

In the 1950s Chip had taken Birney along on one of his many world excursions. She remembers what she calls the kangaroo caper when Chip was trying to locate a pair of kangaroos to send back for Evie to give to the zoo in Washington.

They were spending a week in the old Sydney Hotel in Australia, and Chip placed an ad in the local newspaper. He said that anyone who might possibly have a pair of

Birney and Chip off on World Tour, 1952

young kangaroos for sale should come to the Grand Hotel Sydney at 8 a.m. on Saturday morning.

Birney recounts that it was a bit after dawn on that Saturday when the manager of the hotel came knocking and calling out to them. Birney answered the door and the manager said:

Mr. Robert! There has been a terrible misunderstanding!

Chip asked what could be the matter, and the manager said there were hundreds of kangaroos all hopping around on the front lawn of the hotel. And Chip told him that he had placed an advertisement in the paper. The manager went berserk and told Chip to come quickly down to the lawn. Birney recalls that it was a sight to see. So many people with their kangaroos. The animals were juggling balls, pushing carts, pulling wagons, and even kangaroos with boxing gloves sparring with each other! Finally, Chip did select the kangaroos and they were properly taken all the way back to the Washington Zoo where they found a very good home with several other kangaroos.

In 1965, Evie was stricken with a horrible illness and for several months she was on the verge of death. She was suffering with renal failure and remained hospitalized until she could regain her strength. Eventually, the specialists at the George Washington Hospital diagnosed her with Bright's Disease and she began dialysis treatments, which would continue the rest of her life. This painful and debilitating kidney disease was somewhat slowed by her treatments on an artificial kidney two times each week. She and Chip had donated a machine to the hospital in Washington and when they were in Atlanta she took the dialysis treatments at Grady Memorial Hospital, a building that Chip's firm had designed in the 1950's.

She suffered greatly and continued to weaken. She went with Chip to their farm near Warrenton, Virginia to be with him on his birthday on September 3, 1972. When they arrived back to Washington she was feeling so unwell that they went straight to the hospital. She passed away with her daughter and husband by her side on September 6, 1972.

With the ending of Evie's life a great light had gone out for Chip and he was never able to fully recover from this devastating loss. She had been the great love of his life. It seemed for everyone who knew them, that it was impossible to imagine the end of "Chip and Evie" and their great love affair.

Chip and Evie on the train, 1940's

Chip's son, Major Lawrence Wood Robert, III leading his men before the Battle of the Bulge, 1944

CHAPTER SIX

Chip in Washington Part II–Into World War II

History speaks with a loud voice. Few listen.

Ralph McGill

As Roosevelt's first term drew to a close, Chip became more eager to return to the business of Robert and Company. His firm had grown to one of the largest and most respected engineering and architectural organizations in the Nation and Chip had already stayed longer than he had intended in the Roosevelt Administration.

During these years, Chip kept a humorous story tucked into his files, and folded in his wallet. Composed by an unknown author, it is titled, *Parable of an Engineer*.

One day three men, a lawyer, a doctor, and an engineer, appeared before St. Peter as he stood guarding the Pearly Gates.

The first man to step forward was the lawyer. With confidence and assurance, he proceeded to deliver an eloquent address which left St. Peter dazed and bewildered. The lawyer quickly handed him a writ of mandamus, pushed him aside, and strode through the open portals.

Next came the doctor. With impressive, dignified bearing, he introduced himself. "I am Doctor Brown." St. Peter received him cordially. "Many who preceded you said you sent them here. Welcome to our City."

The engineer had been standing in the background. "I am looking for a job," he said. St. Peter wearily shook his head. "I am sorry," he replied. "We have no work here. If you want a job, you can go to Hell." This response sounded familiar to the engineer. "Very well" he said. "I have had Hell all my life, and I guess I can stand it better than the others."

St. Peter was puzzled. "Look here, young man. What are you?" "I am an engineer." Was the reply. "Oh, yes," said St. Peter. "Do you belong to the Locomotive Brotherhood?" "No," said the engineer. "I am a different kind of an engineer." St. Peter was perplexed and asked him what it was that his type of engineer does. The engineer recalled a definition and replied, "I apply mathematical principles to the control of natural forces." This sounded meaningless to St. Peter, and he let his temper get the best of him. He said, "Young man, you can go to Hell with your mathematical principles and try your hand on some of the natural forces there!" "That suits me. I am always glad to go where there is a rough job to tackle."

And it came to pass that the celestial denizens who had amused themselves in the past by looking down on the less fortunate creatures in the inferno, commenced asking for passes to that other domain. The sounds of agony and suffering were stilled. Many new arrivals, after seeing both places, selected the nether regions for their permanent abode. Puzzled, St. Peter sent messengers to visit Hell and to report back to him. They returned all excited. "That engineer you sent down there has completely transformed the place, He has harnessed the fiery furnaces for light and power. He has cooled the entire place with artificial refrigeration. He has drained the Lake of Brimstone and filled the air with cooled perfumed breezes. He has flung bridges across the Bottomless Abyss, and has bored tunnels through the Obsidian Cliffs. He has created paved streets, gardens, parks and playgrounds. He has created rivers, and lakes, and beautiful waterfalls, That engineer you sent down there has gone through Hell and made it a realm of happiness, peace and industry.

This parable was a testament to how Chip felt about his noble profession.

Chip and Jim Farley planning strategies for the DNC, 1930's

Chip listens to Roosevelt's address, 1934

As Roosevelt entered his second term, having carried every state except Vermont and Maine, the Great Depression was retreating as work programs put more people back to work.

During the 1930s, Chip was still on his crusade to equalize the freight rates for the North and South. Since 1915, he had been relentless in his efforts to further this debate. He continued to argue that there was no reason why these shipping rates should be higher for the Southern States, while they were lower for the Northern States in all instances. For the same materials to be shipped the exact same number of miles, it might be as much as 47 percent more in the South, and Chip had collected years of evidence for his proof.

More than once Chip testified before federal committees to urge that this disparity was not a political issue at all. Rather, it was an issue of economics and equity. His speeches were eloquent and convincing, but nothing seemed to change. He argued that, in the business of commerce, fairness was an unassailable right, not a privilege granted in favor of one party in preference to another.

Finally, Chip decided to try another idea to solve this freight rate issue. In 1937 he founded the Southern Governors Conference which began with seven states and grew to eleven. The primary reason for the annual conference was to discuss freight rate equalization and how the southern states could work together to put pressure on Congress. The governors also discussed the issues of the day that might concern the member states. Chip served as the Executive Director, and was the only member who was not a governor in the Conference.

In his role, Chip arranged all the meetings which always lasted two or three days, and he guided the agendas. During the decades long existence of the Conference, Chip became acquainted with dozens of different governors and learned the many different concerns and difficulties that faced each State.

In addition to trying to solve the freight rate disparity, the Conference had three other major goals:

Checking details for Democratic National Convention at Chicago Stadium, 1940

> To secure uniform tax policies for all areas of business;
>
> To assure friendly labor attitudes between employers and employees; and
>
> To work towards cooperation with the Federal Government regarding major policies affecting the industrial development of the South.

As Chip was readying himself to resign from his position as Assistant Secretary of the Treasury and return to his position at Robert and Company in Atlanta, President Roosevelt and Jim Farley asked him for a meeting. They told Chip that they needed him for the good of the Democratic Party, and they wanted him to serve as Secretary of the National Democratic Committee. Chip decided to accept this honorary volunteer position, and was unanimously elected in 1936 to serve a four year term.

It was obvious to Chip and others in the government that the United States could not avoid the War for much longer. Chip had traveled with the President on a cross country train trip to examine various factories and plants that might be used for the manufacture of war materials. Roosevelt had high expectations about how many planes, ships and tanks the American work force could produce for the war effort, but he knew that it would be years before the United States would be ready to participate in a full-scale war.

Roosevelt's main focus was on the defeat of Adolph Hitler. He also knew that these new factory jobs would provide millions of new jobs for Americans.

Meanwhile, Chip was helping his Party, and getting back to his business. Robert and Company was growing and conducting projects all across the South and Texas. He was still fighting the good fight about the freight rate problem and then out of the blue, he was confronted with accusations that he might be "lobbying" about freight rates, which could be in conflict with his public office of Secretary of the Democratic National Committee. The accusation greatly disturbed Chip. He declared that he was more than willing to testify before Congress, which he did. At these hearings Chip was able to successfully refute all insinuations that his behavior was inappropriate in any way.

Chip reminded the Committee that he had been talking to anybody who would listen for more than twenty-three years about the inequality of freight rates and the problems this disparity was causing for millions of Southerners. Then, Chip reminded the members that his position with the DNC was a purely honorary one and a non-salaried volunteer job. He emphasized that this was a position which he did not seek, but to which he had been unanimously elected, and furthermore, that he was privileged to offer his service.

From there Chip continued on to tell the Committee that he had been fighting for justice and economic fairness for all citizens, not just a few. He emphasized that this rate disparity was not a political issue but a national economic problem that affected every citizen in the United States. Chip testified that a fair rate schedule, equal for all the States, would alleviate much of the struggle the South continued to endure under the present structure.

The Freight Rate issue remained unresolved for several more years. As late as June 23, 1942, just as the Interstate Commerce Commission was preparing to consider this issue which had been on its docket for two and a half years, Congress successfully petitioned for yet another postponement due to World War II. This formal docket item was entitled, "General Class Rate Classification Investigation." It should be noted that some of these rate disparities were as much as 47 percent in favor of the North.

In September of 1943, twenty-one Western and Southern governors joined together with Chip in a public campaign to hold Congress accountable. They held a meeting in Denver for the sole purpose of demanding for Congress to act. Because of this publicity and Chip's relentless efforts, the tariffs were gradually equalized over the entire nation.

It was during this same time that Chip found himself the target of investigation once again. And even though this second inquiry also ended with Chip being exonerated, it did damage to his faith in his fellow man.

It is important to remember that Chip was the very definition of a Washington Outsider and these unfounded accusations were born of jealousy and resentment, neither of which Chip could have expected. It seemed like the politicians were actually envious of his successes and even more, because they could not use any political leverage against an unelected official such as he was.

So, in February of 1939 while Evie was still in the hospital, having just given birth to Birney, Chip rode the Crescent train down to Atlanta to appear before the Georgia Legislature. When he arrived in Atlanta, he issued the following statement:

> *Due to the most recent and past newspaper articles and statements and the apparent misunderstanding on all sides regarding the work being done by Robert and Company, for the state of Georgia at the state sanitarium at Milledgeville and other points in the state, and due further to the ordinary technical perplexities of this whole matter.....I have refrained up to date from injecting myself into this situation but now feel that the time has come when the good name, reputation and business integrity of state officials and people connected with federal governments, as well as those who are called on from the outside business world to do business with such officials and agencies, if possible, be protected from information and insinuations going out to the public, which are very apt to, and in most cases, are destined to create an erroneous impression. Certainly the taxpayers and public have a right to know the facts and have them properly presented. If not, there can certainly be no confidence in government which, I think, is of primary importance.*

Back in August of 1933, an effort began in Georgia to try to secure funds to rehabilitate the crumbling fire hazard that was The Milledgeville State Hospital for the Mentally Ill. The facility was a deathtrap with leaking pipes, paint peeling from the walls, overloaded circuits, and a roof crumbling down. And the worst of all, the hospital was full of patients and trying to operate as a fully functional hospital facility.

At that time, the chief executive was Governor Rivers and he and Chip had known one another for a while. Chip's firm had completed a number of hospital projects, and Chip was especially interested in this hospital in Milledgeville. Chip was born in Monticello, Georgia near Milledgeville and he had known of this facility all his life. He had heard a lot about the problems going back to when his good friend Richard Russell was Georgia's Governor. Eventually, Robert and Company was called in by the State Board of Control and asked to devise a plan for the dilapidated old hospital and sanitarium.

By this time, Roosevelt's New Deal was getting established and the National Recovery Act was working to boost the economy out of the Great Depression. The PWA was earmarking millions of dollars for state government construction projects, and loans were also available from the Reconstruction Finance Corporation (RFC).

Chip was helpful in the filing of all the governmental applications to help the State Board of Control to obtain federal financial aid and apply for a grant. At first, he was unsuccessful, but finally the hospital project won approval and Chip helped arrange the financing through the RFC.

Chip reported that Robert and Company had expended more than $100,000 of its own funds for the preliminary studies involving the hospital. Then, the firm had to make a completely new set of surveys and plans in order to comply with the terms and conditions of the financing forms.

Chip went on to testify that he had a staff of One Hundred Twenty architects, engineers and assistants working day and night, including Sundays, in order to meet every deadline established by the Government. He said that his firm was:

> *The 13th largest in the United States with specialists in every field of engineering and architecture, which naturally made for good savings for the client. We have worked tirelessly to complete this beautiful hospital, under budget, and before the deadline. Had my firm not been on this job, you would still not have a hospital.*

Chip went on to testify:

> *This contract has been examined and reexamined by the engineering section of the Reconstruction Finance Corporation and every item has been approved. The terms and conditions of payment outlined therein have been deemed satisfactory as applying to the design and construction standards of the State Hospital Authority of Georgia.*

Under this approval the RFC. advanced $2,200,000 to the State Hospital Authority and thereafter, the Public Works Administration advanced another $1,800,000 for the development.

During all this debate, Georgia's representatives in the US Congress said privately that there was nothing wrong with the Contract, and the Secretary of the Treasury, Henry Morganthau had defended Chip's integrity absolutely. Governor Rivers had approved every section of the contract, including Robert and Company's six percent fee, and the legislature could not get a single professional witness to testify that the six percent fee was excessive. No engineer nor architect in Georgia would say the fee was high. On the contrary, all testimony was to the effect that the fee was normal. The politicians were jealous of Chip's success but still they could not find him guilty of any wrongdoing.

Chip was very frustrated and had written to his father that while he might be able to understand these accusations if they were from Republicans, it hurt him that he had gotten this criticism from his own party members in his very own state. He had just been trying to help with this job for Georgia, and his own Democratic brethren had attacked him.

Captain Robert, Chip's father, was running Robert and Company along with Chip's other partners, while Chip was serving in Washington. The Captain wrote back to try to console his son. He told him to remember that he hailed from a proud and noble Southern family, and that he must stand tall and hold his head high. He cautioned his son to stay focused upon his vision and to 'keep his powder dry.'

Portrait of Chip's father, The Captain

It was Georgia legislator, Delacy Allen who led the charge to pass a resolution in the Georgia House to investigate Robert and Company and Chip Robert. To wit, that Robert and Company's fees were too high on the Milledgeville Hospital project. Chip indignantly denied all charges. He said that if anything, his firm had been grossly underpaid.

Charges and countercharges flew back and forth across the floor of the legislature. Chip dared Allen to waive his legislative immunity, so he could accuse Allen of slander, and Allen challenged Chip to a fist fight at Georgia Tech's stadium, Grant Field. The entire exchange was broadcast on WSB and WAGA the next night.

In the end Chip and his firm were held to be completely innocent of any wrong doing. The new Milledgeville Hospital and Tuberculosis Sanitarium were hailed as the finest in the Nation.

On the celebration of the one year anniversary of the opening of the Milledgeville Hospital, Ivan Allen, Jr. and some other prominent Atlantans prepared a beautiful, leather bound book telling the story of the old and new hospitals, including before and after photographs. The brochure paid special tribute to Robert and Company and Chip personally for:

The countless hours and tremendous energy and attention that they had given over the entire term of the project. Chip was always available to be of service, no matter when he was called.

Chip was determined that no patient should ever again be forced to stay in the old and dangerous building. He wanted all Georgians to have access to mental health facilities that were safe and modern and he hoped Milledgeville would be a place of aid and assistance for all citizens who might find themselves there struggling with mental illness.

This anniversary brochure ends with a poignant quotation from *The Human Mind*, by Karl A. Menninger:

When a trout, rising to bait, gets hooked on a line and begins to find itself unable to swim about freely, it begins to fight, which results in struggles and splashes and sometimes an escape. Often, of course, the situation is too tough for him.

In the same way, the human being struggles with his environment and the hooks that catch him. His struggles are all that the world sees and usually misunderstands them. It is hard for a free fish to understand what is happening to a hooked one.

Sooner or later, however, most of us get hooked. How much of a fight we may have on our hands then depends on the hook, and, of course, on us. If the struggle gets too violent, if it throws us out of the water, if we run afoul of other struggles, we become 'cases' in need of help and understanding.

There are plenty of cases, Heaven knows. Statistics tell us that one out of every twenty of us is, or has been, or will be, in a hospital for mental illness.

Chip traveling with the Military, 1947

CHAPTER SEVEN

A Time For War–
All Hands on Deck

Never in modern history was a war begun with so smashing a victory by one side, and never in recorded history did the initial victor pay so dearly for his calculated treachery.

Samuel E. Morison, writing about Pearl Harbor

In November of 1940, Franklin Delano Roosevelt was once again elected President of the United States, and the Nation was steadily improving from the ravages of the Great Depression. After the election of 1936, Roosevelt had continued to put in place more programs designed to increase the work force and provide safety nets to the disadvantaged. In the Southern parts of the Nation, for the first time, the Democratic Party had become a political power machine. The Solid South had gained by seniority control of some of the most powerful Committees in Congress, and all across the deep South, conditions for business and labor had become the best in history. The Social Security Act was signed in 1935, and President Roosevelt was at the height of his popularity and prestige.

There was, however, a strong national sentiment against any war involvement whatsoever. This isolationist feeling was partly due to the memory of World War I, and partly due to the raw wounds still healing from the Depression of 1929. Roosevelt knew that the time would come when the United States could no longer stay out of the war in Europe, but he also knew that America was not prepared. He knew as well that any pro-war rhetoric might easily cost him the popularity he now enjoyed.

Just days before President Roosevelt's third Inauguration, he gave an address to Congress, which was destined to become one of his most stirring, and surprising, of his political career.

The President began:

*In times like these it is immature–and incidentally–untrue for anybody to brag that an unprepared America, singlehanded, and with one hand tied behind its back, can hold off the whole world....
As a Nation, we may take pride in the fact that we are softhearted, but we cannot afford to be*

softheaded. We must always be wary of those who, with sounding brass and tinkling cymbal, preach the 'ism' of appeasement.

Then the President harkens back to his 'four freedoms.' He spoke of a world founded on four essential freedoms; the freedom of speech and expression; the freedom of every person to worship God in his own way; the freedom from want; and, the freedom from fear. These four freedoms, he stated, should and must apply to any person in any area of the world.

Here, he speaks about an economic bill of rights:

Equality of opportunity for youth and for others; Jobs for those who can work, security for those who need it; the ending of special privilege for the few; the preservation of civil liberties for all. The enjoyment of the fruits of scientific progress in a wider and constantly rising standard of living.

Chip and his son, Lawrence, 1944

For Chip Robert, there could be no doubt that America must make ready to defeat Adolph Hitler and the growing menace of Germany. He was busy with meetings in Washington, and trying to help with the war effort in any way possible. Chip was receiving a growing number of letters, telegrams and calls, all pleading with him for help. At the beginning of 1938, numerous friends of Chip's had lost touch with their families in Germany and Poland. His friends from New York could get no reply from their relatives, and they had not heard from some friends for months. Of course, Chip, working with Cordell Hull in the State Department, made every effort possible to locate these missing persons, especially in Germany. The sad and horrible truth was soon to be revealed. Hitler's Third Reich had begun the unimaginable massacres of the Holocaust.

All during these months, Roosevelt was in almost daily contact with Winston Churchill. He wanted to help the Prime Minister but was powerless to join the battle. The President saw the destruction of Britain, and so much of Europe, and he knew that the Allies could not long survive. After the Allied defeat at Dunkirk, England was bankrupt, and the situation was becoming desperate. It was clear that Germany was intent upon the conquest of all of Europe.

On June 4, 1940, Prime Minister Churchill appeared before the House of Commons to give a full account of the horrific defeat suffered by the British and French soldiers when they attempted to rescue the Belgians from the German attack at the Port of Dunkirk. The German forces attacked on all sides, especially with their superior air force. They fired with cannon all along the beaches and placed magnetic mines in the channels and seas. The Germans employed their U-boats and motor launches to block the British retreat and this battle lasted for days. Hundreds of British vessels operated day and night attempting to rescue the wounded British, French and Belgians. The Germans then began aiming for the British naval hospital ships. It was a bloodbath.

Churchill continued:

> *[Our losses] were at least four to one, and the Navy, using nearly 1,000 ships of all kinds, carried over 335,000 men....(home) to their native land....We must be very careful not to assign to this deliverance the attributes of a victory. Wars are not won by evacuations....*

Churchill spoke of the Knights of the Roundtable, saying:

> *When every morning brought a noble chance, and every chance brought a noble knight.*

Churchill spoke of the bravery of all the allied soldiers who were:

> *Ready to give life and all for their native land.*

Churchill spoke of the loss not only of men, but of all their weapons and machinery. He reported that everything was lost and:

> *The best we had to give had gone to the British Expeditionary Force....They had the first fruits of all that our industry had to give, and that is gone.*

He goes on to tell the House that he doesn't know how long the fighting forces will have to wait before they can be resupplied, but:

> *Work is proceeding everywhere, night and day, Sundays and week-days. Capitol and labor have cast aside their interests, rights, and customs and put them into the common stock.*

Churchill reminds the Members that this has been a colossal military disaster and that, furthermore, there are rumors that Hitler is planning an attack on London itself.

Then begins the most often quoted, and the most moving part of this famous Dunkirk speech:

> *The British Empire and the French Republic, linked together in their cause and in their need, will defend to the death their native soil, aiding each other like good comrades to the utmost of their strength. Even though large tracts of Europe and many old and famous States have fallen or may fall into the grip of the Gestapo and all the odious apparatus of Nazi rule, we shall not flag or fail. We shall go on to the end. We shall fight in France, we shall fight on the seas and oceans, we shall fight with growing strength in the air, we shall defend our island, whatever the cost may be. We shall fight on the beaches, we shall fight on the landing grounds, we shall fight in the fields and in the streets, we shall fight in the hills, we shall never surrender....*

President Roosevelt was hamstrung by Congress, but he was moving in every way allowed by his Office as President to build up the very small and weak Armed Forces of the United States. On June 11, 1940 Roosevelt signed the appropriation for the gigantic Naval Air Training Center in Corpus Christi Texas, an $85,000,000 project. The race was on. Every effort was put forth to have the most experienced, well-staffed and well-equipped firm in the Nation to be in charge. There was no time for mistakes, and no time to take chances. Everyone in the military, and in particular, the Navy, knew of the sterling reputation of Chip Robert and his firm.

Chip had been doing business with the Navy since the 1920's, and he had grown close to this branch of the military due to the work he had done since WWI to establish the Navy presence at Georgia Tech. Chip knew how crucial this project was for the War effort, and he was more than willing to take on the task. Immediately, the contract was signed and Robert and Company was named Chief Engineers for the building of the Naval Air Training Center in Corpus Christi, Texas. More than 200 of the firm's employees left for Texas to try and make the seemingly impossible happen, so that America could be ready for war as soon as possible.

The very first office structures were built in ten days. The cafeteria served 8,000 men and women, and the hospital had 30 beds and a staff of nurses and doctors. The railroads were custom-built so as to bring in more than 17,000 carloads of supplies, and the original work force was 9,000. In the formal organizational chart for this project, Commander L.N. Moeller was listed as Officer-in-Charge, with Robert and Company named to his immediate right.

Chip was organizing so that an adequate number of his employees could move to Corpus Christi immediately Robert and Company had recently completed Naval Air Projects at Pensacola, Florida and in Puerto Rico. The firm had also done work at the Jacksonville Naval Station, Banana River and Green Cove Springs, all in Florida. The firm was ready and able for this huge project.

It is difficult to express the expansiveness of the Naval Air Training Center, but the statistics contained below will give a general idea.

Corpus Christi, 1942

The area encompassed more than 2,000 acres of beach and sand dunes and through this sandy, bug infested, hot terrain, the work began.

First, there was the laying of 50 miles of rail roads, 115 miles of sewers, 265 miles of electrical systems and paved runways equivalent to an asphalt strip 50 feet wide and 280 miles long.

After the sand dunes were leveled along the shoreline, two miles of steel pilings were sunk to form a retaining bulkhead. Then the giant seaplane hangers were built, each costing a half million dollars.

Everyone at Corpus Christi was committed to creating a fully operational base as quickly as possible. A paving crew was laying a half mile of concrete 22 feet wide every day.

There were 40 cranes, 22 bulldozers, three dredges, two steam locomotives and 440 trucks, all operating on 24 hour schedules. One engineer said that the bulldozers were racing so fast in and out of the great clouds of dust that they looked like tanks in the heat of battle. It was amazing how the trucks kept from hitting one another as they traveled, all day and night, up and down the highway at 50 mph.

Through the end of 1940, every team and every employee had been working straight for six months in 24 hour work rotations, seven days a week, without a break. It was announced that Christmas Day would be a holiday for all. For Thanksgiving the month before, Chip had a big feast delivered to every employee at their work station, but they actually had to eat while they worked, such was the necessity of this job. But, on Christmas Day, even though it was a day off, the whole place became filled up with men and women determined to get some work done. It was a time of great patriotism and pulling together. Truly, everyone was "all in" for their Country.

Construction continued even as the first class of pilots began to train. The mud, sand, mosquitos, and nearly unbearable heat were relentless. One Navy trainee said that when they were on the runways and the sand was swirling all around, the boys would joke that they believed they had been sent to the Foreign Legion. The Corpus Christi Station would now be turning out a class of more than 1,000 aviators each month.

The crew later built a chapel, library, a 1,500-seat auditorium, and a cadet recreation center. The Assembly Repair Department covered fifteen acres and eventually doubled in size. There were swimming pools, a commissary, an officers' club and a gymnasium. Barracks were built for the Marines and WAVES. There was a post office, cafeteria, power plant, laundry, dispensary, dental department, and other buildings, combined to create a self-supporting Naval base.

All hands were exhausted by the ongoing pace of work, but everything continued ahead of schedule. On July 31, 1941, there were 357 officers, 978 aviation cadets, 1,407 enlisted men, and 14 civil service employees on the staff of the station. On November 1, 1941, the first class of

Savannah Port Authority, Robert and Company

Robert and Company on site at Corpus Christi Station, 1942

aviation cadets were graduated and became either ensigns of the US Naval Reserve or second lieutenants in the Marine Corps Reserve.

On August 11, 1943, the work of Robert and Company and the construction company, BBC, was finished. They were awarded the highest possible commendation for excellence by the Army and Navy. Admiral Benjamin Moreel presented a special citation to Robert and Company which reads as follows:

> *The Bureau of Yards and Docks, Navy Department commends Robert and Company for outstanding services rendered, and for their devotion and unswerving fidelity to the tasks at hand when preparing for the Naval Air Station facilities and landing fields in furtherance of the Navy War construction program.*

The Bureau of Yards and Docks Navy Department

Commends

Robert and Company, Incorporated

For outstanding services rendered— Their devotion and unswerving fidelity to the tasks in hand when preparing Plans and Specifications for Naval Air Station Facilities and Landing Fields in furtherance of The Navy War Construction Program

B. Mauell
Chief, Bureau of Yards and Docks

This 29th day of March 1943

Chip's firm is given the ultimate award for excellence by the U.S. Navy, 1943

Captain C.A. Phillips, US Marine Corps wrote that:

> *Corpus Christi was glowing proof that American materials, molded by American factories and machines, under the design of American engineers, set up by American workmen, all together produce a job which cannot be equaled by the resources of any country or combination of countries in the world.*

Of the young soldiers who received their training at Corpus Christi, Captain Phillips reported:

> *Those cadets graduated as aviators in that first class of 1941 were trained in time to take part in the Battles of Midway, the Solomons and others in the South Pacific Theater of War. They were a part of American forces that destroyed Japanese planes and warships to check a hostile naval power that threatened Hawaii, Australia and the whole western hemisphere.*
>
> *Great or small their contribution, these men were a part of the United States Navy that turned back the enemy onslaught. The stakes were not millions nor billions of dollars, but nations and continents.*

And then, on a quiet Sunday morning, everything changed in a cataclysmic way. On December 7, 1941, the Japanese air and sea forces attacked the United States Pacific Fleet at Pearl Harbor.

An incredibly powerful account of this day was written to commemorate the 10th Anniversary of the attack. It was produced by the Public Information Office, Commander in Chief, Pacific and U.S. Pacific Fleet, Pearl Harbor, Territory of Hawaii. Some excerpts from this pamphlet are described as follows:

> *At Dawn on Sunday, December 7, 1941, while Japanese emissaries were negotiating with U.S. officials in Washington, a Japanese task force of 33 ships steamed to a position about 200 miles to the north of Oahu. Three hundred and fifty-three Japanese carrier based air craft were launched in an attack upon the U.S. Pacific Fleet in Pearl Harbor...Japanese planes struck Wheeler Field....then swung to the eastward striking Bellows Field and the Kaneohe Naval Air Station. This wave of aircraft was then split to hit, simultaneously, grounded aircraft at the Naval Air Station on Ford Island, in Pearl Harbor, the Army Air Base at Hickam Field, and the Naval Air Station at Barber's Point....*
>
> *At 8 a.m. another flight of torpedo planes attacked from the east. This allowed time for high-level bombers approaching from the south, over the entrance of Pearl Harbor, to drop their bombs and clear the area for the torpedo runs from the east...The second attack came at 8:40 a.m. from the northeast...and consisted of dive bombers, high-level bombers and fighter aircraft.*

In less than an hour, most of the entire Pacific Fleet had been obliterated, and more than 3,000 servicemen had lost their lives. The history of this tragic day is well documented, as well as the impact this attack had on the outcome of World War II.

Samuel Morison wrote in his *History of United States Navel Operations in World War II*:

> *Never in modern history was a war begun with such smashing a victory by one side, and never in recorded history did the initial victor pay so dearly for his calculated treachery.*
>
> *The bitter war in the Pacific formally ended on the quarterdeck of the battleship* USS Missouri *in Tokyo Bay on September 2, 1945, when representatives of a totally defeated Japanese Empire signed the terms of unconditional surrender.*

On January 5, 1942, the President delivered his third State of the Union Address, in which he announced his goals for arms production acceleration to gear up for the coming full scale war:

> *Plans have been laid here and in the other capitals for the coordinated and cooperative action by all the United Nations—military action and economic action...Already we have established, as you know, unified command of land, sea and air forces in the southwestern pacific theater of war ...Gone forever are the days when aggressors could attack and destroy their victims one by one without unity of resistance. We of the United Nations will so dispose our forces that we can strike at the common enemy wherever the greatest damage can be done him. The militarists of Berlin and Tokyo started this war, but the massed, angered forces of common humanity will finish it.*

In September 1942, with the United States in full war production, and the whole Country unified to defeat the Axis powers, Chip joined in a special train trip along with a group of Roosevelt's close associates on a coast to coast journey. The sole purpose of this trip was to inspect plants, factories and ship yards already in production of war machinery. Roosevelt had already projected what he believed the output could be, but most people believed it to be utterly impossible to achieve. Americans wanted the President to succeed, but how could it possibly be?

President Roosevelt wanted to increase the production rate of airplanes to 60,000 in 1942 and 125,000 in 1943. He asked for 45,000 tanks with increase to 75,000 in 1943. And, as for shipping, he wanted to increase production to 6,000,000 deadweight tons. It seemed a super human task, but Americans rose to the challenge.

As President Roosevelt's train rolled across America, he stopped for dozens of inspections, most of which were unannounced. In Detroit, factories had been converted to produce 30 tanks a day; the new Willow Run Ford facility was turning out one new B24 bomber plane every 63 minutes; the new Boeing Plant in Seattle was finishing 362 B 17 Flying Fortress aircrafts every month; and while the train was at the Kaiser Ship Building Yard in Oregon, Roosevelt's daughter Anna christened the new 10,000 ton freighter, the *USS Joseph Teal* which had been built in only ten days. The new age of assembly line mass production had become the way of manufacturing in America. Over 18,000,000 men and women were employed now in the United States for wartime production, more than six times the total number of new jobs during the whole era of the Depression.

One of the many projects which was designed and engineered by Robert and Company was the historic Bell Bomber Plant, now the site of Lockheed Georgia, located in Marietta. Chip was personally involved with all aspects of this work and Robert and Company not only handled the engineering requirements for the project, but also, in conjunction with the U.S. Army Corps of Engineers, supplied complete management and supervisory services during the entire construction project.

On March 16, 1943, the members of the Georgia State Legislature visited the facilities and Chip made the following remarks:

> *It is a great pleasure to have you as our guests on this the greatest war project yet undertaken by our Government. Ground was broken for this project on March 31, 1942, and since that time, we have completely designed and constructed what you are about to see today....We have delivered, as of yesterday for beneficial occupancy the main assembly building, and within 30 days this entire project will be practically completed....The Government has placed this project in our*

Ground breaking for Bell Bomber Plant, March 30, 1942

State with a feeling that it will be a success in every way. The upwards of 30,000 employees on this gigantic project are to come from Atlanta and this vicinity, and it will not encroach on other vital war industries and activities. It behooves us to see that this is properly done. This is primarily why you have been invited to see just what the Government has put in our midst and to carry the word back home of the job that is up to all of us.

After your visit, I am sure you will fully realize the tremendous task involved and what a great part this project is designed to play in bringing this war to a successful close. In the peace to come, I can visualize that the additional labor that this great enterprise will use will absorb almost entirely our peacetime unemployment in this vicinity, a thing we have always wished and hoped and labored for. It is up to us to make it a reality.

Captain Harry L. Collins, Vice President of Bell Bomber Manufacturing Company in Buffalo New York, was the official in charge of the Marietta plant. The Company published a monthly magazine and in the April, 1943 issue there appeared an article about the Marietta plant:

It was exactly a year ago, March 30, 1942, that Army engineers moved into the area and started breaking ground for one of the largest air craft plants in the world. Official title of the facility is the "Marietta Aircraft Assembly Plant," but to the enthusiastic people...of the surrounding community, it is...the Bell Bomber plant.

What was once a rolling, wooded countryside, soon resembled a huge ant hill as thousands of men and machines started to level off the nearly 3,000 acre area. Soon, deep depressions for the huge building foundation became evident. Miles of highway were constructed. Huge parking lots were laid out to handle heavy traffic when 25,000 to 40,000 workers move in to take their places in Bell Bomber's Production Army. In all, some 9,000,000 cubic yards of red Georgia clay were moved to make way for the plant and facilities, The main factory is a half mile long and a quarter mile wide. Windowless, with a flat roof...two empire state buildings could be laid end to end inside the factory with space left over for a baseball diamond. A dozen football fields placed goal post to goal post could be placed across its width. The door to get the bombers out of the factory is seven stories high. Two railroad tracks extend from one end of the factory to the other for efficient movement of supplies. More than 2,300 dwellings were built at a cost of $9,000,000 to house all the workers who did not come from the immediate area. These are the workers who are here in a supervisory capacity who will be sent down from Buffalo, New York.

And so it was that this major assembly plant was completely finished, from cotton field to the first bomber off the lines, in 18 months. A nearly heroic feat... and, the very first plane was christened 'The Yellow Jacket.'

Even during these very busy and trying years, Chip never neglected his beloved alma mater. He was always involved on the Georgia Tech Athletic Board, and served on the State of

Showing new C5A, former Bell Bomber Assembly Plant, Marietta, Georgia

Georgia Board of Regents (when the Board of Trustees was supplanted by the new Board) and he continued to help out in any way he could. In 1942, he gave a parcel of property to Georgia Tech, located on 3rd Street between Williams and Techwood Drive, which was key to Tech's master building plan. He continued to help deserving students with their tuition expenses, and he tried his best to attend every Tech football game. Chip was always interested in anything that concerned football or baseball. A reporter for the *Los Angeles Examiner*, Vincent Flaherty, wrote about how he and Chip would have long conversations over the years about baseball and back during World War II, Chip had scolded Vince and the other sports writers about their criticism of the wartime baseball players. Chip, to some extent, blamed the reporters for the public's lack of interest about war time baseball:

Everybody knows that the players are not as good as the prewar stars. But that's not the point. You (sportswriters) have done nothing toward putting the impression across that the games are just as interesting as ever...Baseball is baseball, and a darned interesting game, whether it is played by sandlot kids, college minor leaguers, or big league talent. Everything being equal, a ball game makes for a nine inning contest....Unquestionably, (the players now) don't do things as well as the DiMaggio's and Feller's, but...they are trying just as hard and giving all they have...and that's all one could ask.

Even though Chip had long ago turned down the invitation by Ty Cobb to join the Detroit Tigers, he was always a big fan of baseball. For several years Chip, and several other prominent Atlantans, owned the now defunct Atlanta Crackers team which played in the old field on Ponce de Leon Avenue beginning in the early 1900's.

Ironically, as the United States was preparing to enter World War II, there had been another battle raging in Washington. And this stormy war was all about Chip Robert. Once again, Chip and his firm were the targets of another investigation and this time in the United States Congress. The charge was simply that Robert and Company was getting work with the Government, and that since Chip was the Secretary of the Democratic National Committee, this just might be a conflict of interest for his firm. At first, Chip was amazed and angered, and quick to rise to the challenge. He had just been unanimously reelected to a second four-year term at the Democratic Convention in Chicago, and he certainly did not want to abandon his Party. He reminded the Committee, convened by Senator Bridges, that his position was an honorary one with no salary or privileges attached, and he saw no reason why he should abandon his post since he had never been a quitter. Chip went on to say that the generals and admirals with the armed forces had actively sought him out for these various government jobs. They knew his firm, and knew Robert and Company could be trusted to do the job correctly and deliver a first-class product with all due haste. He furthermore accused the Senator of trying to clog up the war effort. During the investigation, the Naval, Marine and Army Officers were quick to come forward to testify on Chip's behalf. They said they needed these bases and stations, and they needed them fast. The officers all wanted the expertise, integrity and commitment of Robert and Company especially since speed was imperative to be able to enter the War effort and time was in such short supply. As the days and weeks continued, Chip realized that his only choice was to resign his post in the Democratic Party rather than to put any possible shadow upon the President's upcoming run for reelection. This, even though Chip had been cleared of any wrongdoing. On September 22, 1940, Chip delivered the following letter to Roosevelt at Hyde Park on September 22, 1940:

My Dear Mr. President,

I herewith enclose a copy of the letter I am delivering tomorrow to Ed Flynn, which letter speaks for itself. I am sure you know me well enough down through the years to know that I fully recognize the exigencies of these times and that I will never be found outside the front line trenches. In resigning at this particular time, I do so with the fullest feeling that our present campaign will have but one outcome—complete success. I have traveled far and wide over the Country since the Chicago Convention and I have gained this definite impression from personal contacts and connections on every hand. I have highly enjoyed being associated with your Administration, and I take this occasion to express to you my loyalty and sustained devotion.

Respectfully yours,
Chip Robert

Chip's letter of resignation to Ed Flynn states, in part:

At a time like the present, I cannot serve the best interests of my Company and also the best interests of my party connections simultaneously, and there cannot and must not be a conflict between the two.

Chairman Flynn said that he accepted Mr. Robert's resignation with the greatest of regrets. So, Chip resigned and set about to move full throttle into the business of his firm producing a prodigious amount of work for the war effort, as well as a great number of civil work projects and municipal jobs throughout the south.

But then, after all these unfounded accusations that Chip had been made to endure, yet another committee wanted to investigate his government work again in 1943. This time, the House Naval Affairs Committee wanted an investigation to find out if Robert and Company had been getting too much governmental work. The news headlines read, "$7,000,000 in war fees paid to firm of 'Chip' Robert up to 1943." But, here again, all of these accusations and inquiries came to naught. The Committee determined that Chip had done nothing improper.

The next day an article was published in the *Washington Times Herald* by columnist Frank C. Waldrop. Titled 'Soak the Successful.' The writer said:

That was a cheap and dirty piece of business that the House Committee on Naval Affairs turned in Friday, smearing the architectural and engineering firm headed by Chip Robert of Atlanta and Washington. It just demonstrates once more that in these days, the sure way to get yourself plastered and smeared is to have ability, and to use it.

Chip Robert is known not only throughout Washington, but all over the United States as an able citizen. His company is one of the largest engineering organizations in the United States—which means the World. For the past four years…Robert…has been building air bases, factories, and war plants all through North America….The Army and Navy have given Robert and Company *commendation upon commendation, and letters of praise about every job. More than that, they have kept on coming back to him for jobs. But still the House Naval Affairs Committee, Friday, tried to make this case seem other wise. Their own report shows that the Army and the Navy have given Robert and Company over $305,794,415 worth of construction work for the war and are still planning more work with that firm.*

Now, why is that?

Do they hand Chip multimillion dollar contracts because he is a guy with a sparkling personality?

Do they think he can deliver the goods with a winning smile?

Anybody with any sense knows perfectly well the real reason. The United States Army and Navy keep coming back to Chip Robert with work ONLY because he can do what they want done.

But when a smear session opens up in Congress and downtown among the Washington Sharpshooters, the facts have a hard time coming out. In this city, the official slogan is "soak the successful", and Chip Robert has committed the crime of being successful.

For instance, the sharpshooters screeched that (Chip) came to Washington to take a government job at $7,000 a year in 1933, and in 1942, he was drawing down $189,184 from his company....Like many another able citizen, Chip Robert he might have a whirl at public affairs one day...and Roosevelt gave him his chance.

He made a mistake in so doing. For like many another able citizen, all he has ever got since his whirl with public affairs is a headache. (The excellence of his firm has a proven record) and his company's earnings average 2.43% of the cost of the contract. This is phenomenally low and the government would be doing a terrific job with taxpayers' money if all the rates were like that.

But Robert is successful. So he gets soaked. A Committee of Congress rakes and hauls his books from front to back, and finally turns in a report that hints and sniggers, but on examination, only proves that Robert and Company has served this Country well.

In this Country, men of ability used to be looked up to for doing such work, and if they made money, well, that was the American Way and everybody hoped to do as much himself, someday.

But now, do your work and your reward is a slap in the face by some branch of the government. Why in the hell do the American people stand for this sort of thing anyhow?

It is not difficult to imagine how disappointing all of this was to Chip, and how disheartening for him. But, even after such poor treatment and lack of appreciation by his fellow Americans, his heart was still not hardened. For just as peace was restored in Europe, and the hard fought fight had been won, Chip was about to be called to serve his Country yet another time. And the coming effort would prove to be one of the most significant endeavors of his entire professional life.

CHAPTER EIGHT

Post-War Europe: The Marshall Plan and More Than Half a Million Miles

Let your trip, as near as you can, be in the nature of a good will journey, building up closer relationships between the United States and all the foreign countries you touch. In other words, be most cordial and friendly and make them think a great deal of you personally and of America in general.

Chip Robert, 1935—advice to a young traveler

During the 1940s, Robert and Company was involved in massive Government War projects as well as civil engineering jobs all across the United States and overseas. The firm was continuing to grow, and Chip was making his headquarters as much in Atlanta as in Washington. He was traveling constantly, and seemed to thrive on visiting foreign lands.

Franklin Delano Roosevelt passed away on April 12, 1945 at his beloved Warm Springs, Georgia, just a few months short of being able to rejoice in the final Allied victory, for which he had worked so tirelessly throughout the brutal war years. Harry S. Truman became the 33rd President of the United States, the Nazi regime in Germany was defeated, and on September 2, 1945, the Japanese Government formally surrendered on the deck of the battleship *USS Missouri* in Tokyo Bay.

By 1946, unemployment in America was below four percent and the Nation began an era of prosperity, confidence, and renewed optimism and hope for the future. There was a strong consensus that America would never again be an 'isolationist' country, and everyone seemed interested in helping Europe to rebuild.

By 1947, The United States was well on its way to becoming the new superpower of the World. The 'Cold War' against Russia was emerging and Americans rallied around the new Truman Doctrine, which had as its mission, the absolute containment of the spread of Communism, and a total mistrust of Russia.

Secretary of State, General George C. Marshall, speaking in 1947 at Howard University, said that political stability and world peace depended upon a fast return to normal economic health. The Marshall Plan proposed massive military aid to help Europe in peacetime to rebuild, not just it's infrastructure but also its economy.

Subsequently, sixteen nations met in Paris to set their goals. They asked for aid from the United States in the amount of $22 billion. America was committed to help with the reconstruction of Europe in any way possible. During 1947, President Truman asked all Americans to take part in 'meatless' Tuesdays and 'no poultry' Thursdays in a grand effort to help provide food for the starving masses of Europe.

1948 was an election year and the first presidential election in 16 years without Roosevelt on the ballot. The Republicans, convening in Philadelphia, nominated Thomas E. Dewey for President with Earl Warren to be his Vice President. The Democrats, also meeting in Philadelphia, nominated Harry S. Truman with Alben Barkley as Vice President.

President Truman won a hard fought battle that year, and Chip had played a major role in the victory. During the years when Truman had been Senator and then as Vice President and President, Chip had become close personal friends with the President and his wife and daughter and had always stayed in close contact with them long after Harry Truman had passed away. Chip enjoyed his trips to Missouri to visit all of the family, from time to time.

It was not long after Truman became president in 1945, that he began talks with Chip about the reconstruction of war-torn Europe and the part Chip might play. At that time, Chip was one of the most widely traveled private citizens in the United States. In addition to Chip's knowledge of world affairs, he had superior experience in building and engineering which could be most helpful in analyzing the needs of Europe. It was in this context that Chip agreed to serve as envoy and special delegate to travel and assess the world condition, and to make reports and recommendations back to the President.

And so it came to pass that Chip Robert purchased the very first around-the-world Ticket from Pan American World Airways, for his global trip in September, 1947.

Evie's mother, who had been recently widowed, hosted an elegant bon voyage party for him at their mansion in Washington, DC and Chip left from there to catch the midnight train to New York City and then travel directly to Dallas, Texas for several meetings. From there, he flew to Los Angeles and San Francisco and stayed a week, meeting with officials of the military, and reuniting with some longtime college friends. Next, he was off to Hawaii for a series of tours of the islands, and conferences with members of the Armed Forces.

Post-War Europe: The Marshall Plan and More Than Half a Million Miles

Chip off to London, 1950's

American Airways early flights

Early air travel, Eastern Airlines

Chip with Jim Farley, air travel, 1930's

When he set off on a military transport for his arduous nine hour flight to Guam, Chip knew that he was really on his way.

Chip believed that World War II was not over, but that it had turned into an economic war all across Europe. Even though the bombing had ended, destruction and misery were common everywhere. Chip believed that these remnants were the greatest tragedies of war. He thought that it was the responsibility of the victors to return to the defeated nations and extend the hand of cooperation. He believed that the foundation of the Marshall Plan called for the United States to offer assistance wherever possible to the stricken populations.

During his first trip of 40,000 miles and 28 nations, he visited every country which had been affected by the War. As he traveled through the world, he found that in all countries, there was a feeling of great good will towards the United States. The United States had actually taken the place of Great Britain as the leader of the free world. It was always Chip's feeling that America's new predominant place in the world order was brought about by the power of democracy.

During his trips Chip had many long and intimate conversations with General Douglas MacArthur and General Lucius Clay. All three of these men believed that the success of the recovery of Europe would be a huge victory for the United States. The armed forces were already doing remarkable work in Japan and Germany, and Chip was greatly anticipating his first visit to these countries since the war.

It is important to note that Chip was sixty years old when he began making the global trips for the State Department. After he made his first trip for the US Government and as he began traveling between Hong Kong and Cairo more often, the State Department thrust more and more duties upon him. All totaled, Chip made seventeen around-the-world trips and this was during an era when traveling by air was not very comfortable and certainly much slower than today. Also, these special fact-finding journeys do not include his destination trips just to London or Paris, and back to the United States afterwards, and these shorter trips were in addition to his around-the-world trips.

Chip's usual method when going around the world was to purchase a base ticket from Pan American. Then he did many thousands of miles as add-ons, using military transport planes as well as British Airways, Royal Dutch Airline, Chinese National, Air India, TWA, Air France, Norwegian Air, and Northwest Airlines. For example, he flew Pan Am from Guam and Manilla to Bangkok and then to Siam, and did not pick back up with Pan Am until Lisbon. He then flew Pan Am to the Azores, Gander, Newfoundland and down the North Atlantic Coast, arriving back home to New York, in late October.

On Chip's first trip, he had extensive tours of the war damage in Germany. He had arrived in London and General Clay sent his plane to take Chip straight to Berlin. He landed expecting poor conditions, but he was totally unprepared for the destruction of the city. Chip had traveled to Berlin several times in the 20s and 30s but could not find a single landmark to help him get his bearings. All he could see was miles and miles of debris. The great Brandenburg

Chip headed to Paris, 1940's

Gate was rubble, the famous Adlon Hotel was obliterated, and the Tiergarten had literally disappeared. Chip was walking among the German people who were plodding along in a dazed bewilderment. All public transportation had been destroyed in the War and he called the atmosphere desolate.

The American Army of Occupation was employing thousands of German civilians. They were working for very low wages but the Army provided a large hot lunch in the middle of the day. Thousands more were waiting to be hired and were eager to work even for no pay as long as they could have a meal. The army also gave the office workers extra food because they were so starved that they fell asleep at their desks by early afternoon. Chip had been eager to see Germany again but after he witnessed the destruction, he could hardly wait to leave.

On his tour of Germany, Chip was flown to Munich, Stuttgart, Manheim, Frankfurt, Wiesbaden, Dachau, Heidelberg, and Berchtesgaden. At Nuremberg, he was permitted to attend the war crimes trials for a day. He met with the judges who he had known before the war, and they authorized him to observe the trials of the SS officers who had managed some of the prison camps as well as some of the gas chambers.

Chip was given a special tour of Normandy, France in order that he could see first hand the damage from D Day. He was guided through the Utah and Dakota beach heads, and he was very moved by the experience. He saw thousands of war machines, half sunk along the beaches; boats and tanks rusting away; and artillery canons stuck in the sand. In the years that followed, Chip said that every American who is able, should visit Normandy and view the thousands upon thousands of unmarked crosses at the special memorial cemetery.

One leg of this first trip was spent in India and Egypt and this too was a revelation for Chip. While it was true that India and Egypt had not suffered much damage during the war, there was civil war raging everywhere. Over a half billion Indians were fighting and killing one another. And the same thing was happening in Egypt. It was not safe to even venture out in the streets. Chip believed that Great Britain had withdrawn from these nations too abruptly. He thought that the local governments should have been turned over more gradually, so that the citizens could have had a chance to learn the responsibilities of their new freedom to become a democracy.

There were many cities which were too dangerous for Chip to visit in 1947. These included New Delhi, Bombay and Columbo. He was able to visit Agra to see the majestic Taj Mahal which he called the acme of perfection and beauty. And he said that the palace was even more beautiful in the moonlight than in the daytime.

On one afternoon, Chip set forth with a driver while he was in Calcutta. He knew that Mahatma Gandhi was scheduled to make an appearance to urge for peace and he wanted to be a witness. During that September of 1947, Gandhi had come out from under his fast in an effort to quell the rioting taking place between the Hindus and the Muslims. The grounds around the National Administration Building were packed with Indians of all ages. The weather was desperately hot, sweltering and damp and the crowd must have reached 250,000 at least. Chip was able to get within 30 feet of Gandhi's raised platform and he was able to see very clearly what was going on. Chip reported that the atmosphere was the most amazing thing he had ever seen. He said the throngs of people grew absolutely still and quiet and that you could hear a pin drop. There was such reverence for this holy man and one could tell the crowd was hanging on his every word. Gandhi begged his people to stop their warring against one another, but after his speech, the tragic massacres resumed the very next day.

In Egypt, Chip observed the similar type civil wars all around the country. His pilot flew into the Cairo at sunset and Chip tells in his diary of the gorgeous reds and oranges of the sunset, and of the vista of the sphinx and pyramids right below. Chip stayed at Shepherds Hotel and thought Cairo was very similar to New York City. He took the time to ride around the pyramids on a camel, and he did have a welcome break with a sightseeing trip to Alexandria, about one hundred fifty miles from Cairo. He had been invited to an oasis near the Mediterranean which was owned by a wealthy Egyptian. There were camels provided for the journey up to the site

Chip in Egypt, 1947

of the party, huge tented banquet areas, exotic dancers and a sumptuous luncheon was served in Chip's honor. He enjoyed every minute.

From Egypt, Chip flew to Greece. He had been to Athens several times in the past and thought the city was in very good shape. But as he was chauffeured through the countryside he saw that everything was in upheaval. The railroads were mostly destroyed and every highway was in shreds because, as the Nazis retreated, they had done as much damage as possible.

He also flew to Basra, Damascus and Jerusalem. When he landed at noon in The Holy Land, the temperature was one hundred twenty-one degrees in the shade. When it was time for their departure, Chip rode in the cockpit with the pilot. They circled the Suez Canal and headed eastward towards England.

This 1947 trip was Chip's first visit to London since his wartime marriage to Evie in October of 1935. He was shocked when he checked into his favorite hotel, the Dorchester. The grand old hotel was open for business, but it was far from grand. The rooms were dilapidated and there was hardly any food to be had. Chip was served kippered herring for his breakfast meals and Brussels sprouts with potatoes for every lunch and dinner. This certainly made an impression upon Chip, and strengthened his conviction that America must do much more than the Marshall Plan originally provided. He believed that if the United States failed to provide support, then all of Europe would fall to the Soviets.

Throughout Chip's daily dairies, he speaks of his love of flying and of how he thought it was superior to any other form of transportation. He is often trying to convince his friends of the safety of airplanes and the value of saving time. When he was flying into Naples on one of his trips, the pilot leveled the plane at 5,000 feet and then took Chip directly down into the crater of the Vesuvius Volcano. On all sides of the plane, Chip could see the red hot lava boiling around him, and he could see the yellow color from the gases deep inside the crater. Chip said it was one of the great thrills of his trip.

When Chip returned to Atlanta, he gave many talks about his trip around the world. People always asked if he was afraid to fly in the small planes over long stretches across the oceans and desolate mountain ranges. Here is his reply:

> *As far as I am concerned, and I do knock on wood, that instead of having my friends and family standing around to give me the last slug of glucose and digitalis, I would far rather have the report come back that, along the timberline of a certain mountain range way off yonder, they found in the ashes, a Georgia Tech football captain's ring of the vintage 1908, and therefore, it must have been me at last.*

One of the paramount reasons for this 1947 trip was for Chip to make a close examination of Japan. This portion of his trip could make a book in itself. He recalls that as his plane drew close to land, his pilot made a special effort to circle Mount Fuji several times at an altitude of 10,000 feet. He said this was spectacular. Chip had been assigned a special military escort for this visit to Japan and when his pilot neared Hiroshima, he flew very low over the city so that Chip could get a close aerial view of the destruction. Then they landed so Chip could survey the damage on the ground. Chip spent an entire day assessing what Japan would require to rebuild its country. The next day, he visited all day at the Department of Justice, observing the War Crimes trials in progress. Afterwards, he had a forty minute meeting with the prime minister of Japan, which Chip describes as one of the most momentous occasions of his journey.

While staying in Tokyo, Chip had many private visits with General Douglas MacArthur whom he had not seen since they first met in Washington in 1934. The General went out of his way to show Chip around and to make a number of travel arrangements on chartered military planes. MacArthur told Chip that nearly a decade ago, when he was struggling to get funding for the Army, that Chip alone had stood up to the PWA and fought to get a bigger budget for the military. The General said how he would never forget the kindness that Chip had shown that day.

On this 1947 trip, Chip had purchased a ticket for a side trip to China, and this ticket was more expensive than the entire price of the original 'around-the-world' ticket. Chip enjoyed his visit to Shanghai and Peking and took a tour of the Great Wall of China and all the ancient historical sights. He traveled to Chungking and Nanking, and then he was off to fly to Hong Kong and Manila. He especially wanted to see the Bataan Peninsula and Corregidor to try and imagine the horror of these battles in which some of his friends had died.

Chip traveled to Saigon and next to Bangkok where he was wowed by that country's architecture.

It was necessary for Chip to fly on some unconventional aircraft in order to get to all the places he needed to go. Even in the best of circumstances, travel to so many exotic places could be extremely rough. In one of his diaries, he writes the following account:

> *I shall never forget finding myself unsuspectedly on what is known as a bucket seat job of The Royal Dutch Airlines flying between some of the islands of the Far East Indies. A bucket seat job is a transport plane arranged so that all the passengers sit on canvas benches along either side of the plane, with their backs to the walls. Most times, down the middle aisle of the plane, a considerable and varied cargo is strapped to the floor of the plane. I had this sort of transportation two or three times when I changed my schedule and was in a hurry to move.... ON this particular trip in route to Borneo, there was on board a Chinese merchant and his family.... They were carrying three black face ring tailed monkeys and seven parrots. The parrots were cackling and fussing. The monkeys seemed frightened to death once we got higher than the tree tops. The monkeys screamed and shrieked like babies. The parrots clucked like chickens and finally at about 7,000 feet, the monkeys played dead.... It was a tremendous relief to all passengers.*

During Chip's second world trip, he was on a special State Department mission and he made an extensive visit to the Soviet Union. On his flight from Paris to Berlin, Chip was the only civilian passenger on a DC-3 Army transport plane when they had engine trouble. The plane was flying at 10,000 feet toward Berlin when one engine began to sputter and smoke. All the Army personnel, four officers and Chip were ordered to line up at the door of the plane. Chip was the second man in line, and none of the passengers had ever jumped from an airplane.

The order came to 'make ready to jump,' and Chip grabbed his passport and his money. He was regretting having to leave behind his new polaroid camera. Chip's only son, Lawrence, had been a paratrooper in the Battle of the Bulge in 1944 and Chip was trying to remember any tips Lawrence might have mentioned. After a few minutes the second engine began to sputter but the pilot continued trying to repair both of them. Everyone remained in line waiting for the "Go" signal. At last, the pilot was able to get both engines working and the plane landed safely. Later, at the inquiry, the crew testified that Chip was the only one who actually seemed eager to jump!

Over the next twenty years Chip was to visit most every corner of the globe, and log more than 500,000 miles on the world trips alone. His often cited advice was that every traveler should go with plenty of money, good health, and a keen sense of humor.

Touring in Balboa

Chip off on a cruise to the West Indies, 1934

CHAPTER NINE

Circling Back Home

I am just a simple country boy, but in my business, my goal is always to be on time and under budget and always with excellence and integrity in everything we do.

Chip Robert

As time went by, Chip was busier than ever, and his travels remained a regular part of his schedule. It seemed as if the constant motion of the trains and planes were his oxygen, and that he thrived on being in new lands and meeting new people. He preferred to fly whenever he could, which allowed him to go more places in less time and Chip was always in a hurry. Chip firmly believed that air travel was the future and he wanted the South to be a part of this new industry.

Chip's first global trip was in 1947, taking nearly three months and covering 40,000 miles. He had just turned sixty years old. After that journey, he would take sixteen more of these around-the-world trips, not counting all his shorter flights abroad which were focused on just one or two countries. He may have been the most well-traveled civilian of his time.

In Chips professional life, the Atlanta Airport was probably the largest and longest ongoing job that Robert and Company undertook. The role of his firm, in creating the modern Hartsfield-Jackson International Airport, the busiest airport in the world–has had an indelible influence upon the development of Atlanta and the entire Southeast.

In Atlanta in 1929 the 'Candler field airport', built by the Candler family of Coca Cola fame, was just a racetrack, and a great entertainment destination during those years. It was a rough dirt track surrounding a cotton field where a group of auto enthusiasts and their friends sometimes raced cars for fun. This field was approximately where the Atlanta Airport International Concourse is now located.

Chip and his friend Bill Hartsfield, who became Mayor of Atlanta in 1937, often talked about the merits of air transportation and of having a modern air terminal for Atlanta. In those early years Chip was a director and shareholder of the Aviation Corporation of America and he began flying with actor and humorist Will Rogers during the times of the first single propeller airplanes.

When Chip joined the Roosevelt Administration after the 1932 election one of his many duties as Assistant Secretary of the Treasury was to help coordinate some of the relief programs during the Great Depression. He was the official in charge of the PWA program regarding aviation, and in that role, Chip began sending millions of dollars to the Southern States and all over the United States for constructing airstrips and terminal buildings. This was the very beginning of commercial air transportation in America.

In the Roosevelt administration Chip was responsible for the federal grants which were awarded to Atlanta to build the first hard surface runways and other airport structures. Eastern Airlines was the first to haul passengers in and out of Atlanta. Their first planes were the Curtis Condor and the Flying Kingbird which were propeller planes. It was a thrilling time and the rest is history.

Once World War II was over at last, Chip persuaded Mayor Hartsfield to accompany him on an international tour of various airports around the world. Both men had a vision for Atlanta, and both men knew that an international airport would be the centerpiece. They had dreamed of a facility that could serve jet aircraft, offer international destinations, and become a state-of-the-art modern terminal that would be a transportation hub for the entire Southeast. Chip knew what this type of development could do to bring additional industry to the South, and all of the new jobs which would follow. All he had to do was make the case, and he did.

This fun-loving pair of men, Mayor Hartsfield and Chip Robert, adored adventure of any sort. They departed Atlanta in May of 1950 and Chip had arranged all the details. In only sixteen days, they toured London, Paris, Copenhagen, Stockholm, Rome, and Berlin.

A United States Airforce plane transported the men to Berlin where they were met by Captain Richard Lake. Because they had a military escort, Chip and the Mayor were allowed to travel freely about the Russian Sector of the city, and to witness all the restoration being done by the U.S. civilian military.

In Paris, the two had a private tour of the city zoo and other establishments which might be illustrative of the institutions Atlanta hoped to build one day. They spent many hours touring Orly Airport, and then, just as they made ready to depart Paris, all traffic was brought to a standstill because of a pilot strike. Chip was able to purchase tickets on The Orient Express from Paris to Frankfurt and they had a wonderful trip aboard this historic train.

Upon their return to Atlanta, Mayor Hartsfield was asked how they had managed to tour six cities in just sixteen days, He replied, 'The answer is air transportation, good planning, and a wonderful traveling companion.'

Ten years after this historic trip, construction for Atlanta's new airport was underway. Robert and Company had drawn the plans and produced scale models to better illustrate just how the new air terminal would look when it was completed. All the federal, state, and municipal funding was secured for this $19,000,000 project was formally announced on February 3, 1957.

In the 1970s Robert and Company joint ventured the new Midfield Terminal facilities, and so it was, since the days of the cotton field, Robert and Company has been consistently and continuously involved with Atlanta's airports. And today, Robert and Company designs and engineers aviation facilities throughout the world.

By the late 50s and 60s, Chip's firm was designing and engineering hospitals across the United States. Chip had always taken special interest in hospital design all over the world, and he traveled many times to the countries of Scandinavia to study the innovations and techniques used for hospitals in Denmark and Copenhagen. When Robert and Company engineered the modern rotary kiln incinerator for Atlanta, which was the first of its kind built in the United States, the firm had the plans drawn up in Denmark, because a company in that country held the patent. It was during the war years, and Chip tells the story of how difficult and dangerous it was to try and get the plans out of Denmark. In fact, this incinerator project almost had to be abandoned, but Robert and Company was finally able to get the specification drawings out of the Nazi-occupied area and to complete the job for the City of Atlanta.

Grady Memorial Hospital first opened its doors in Atlanta in 1892 and was operated by the City of Atlanta until 1945. Since that time, Grady has been a facility of the Fulton Dekalb Hospital Authority.

Robert and Company was awarded the contract to design and engineer the new Grady Memorial Hospital and on January 26, 1958 this huge new facility was dedicated with the opening remarks by Mayor Hartsfield.

The new 21-story building with rooms for 1,000 beds and 325 bassinets was built at a cost of $26,000,000. Emory University was in charge of the medical personnel, and a visiting staff of 500 Atlanta physicians. There were 110 doctors on the house staff, and all totaled, hospital employees numbered over 1000. There was also a group of 475 volunteers and a full-time chaplain. Chip wrote that the new hospital was beautiful in every way, and would be a source of pride for all of the South. He especially liked the limestone relief carvings of his hero, Henry W. Grady, which had been placed in the lobby of the hospital.

Chip continued to be a delegate at every Democratic National Convention, and because of his work for President Truman, they had developed a friendship which lasted until Truman passed away. During Truman's campaign Chip was always available to help. At one point, when many thought Thomas Dewey might win the election, President Truman and his staff and other Democrats were on his campaign train traveling from coast to coast, urgently trying to get people to listen to his message. The train stopped in Chicago and when it was time to depart, the train refused to move. It seemed that there was a large amount of ticket fares which had not been paid, and this train was supposed to keep on going to the west coast and back again to New York.

Someone aboard the train made a quick call to Chip Robert for help. Chip immediately sent enough money to get the train rolling again. After that Chip raised all the money for the rest of the trip. There was never a time that Chip did not do whatever was in his power to

Monte Carlo, 1950

aid the DNC.

No matter what year it happened to be, if it was Saturday afternoon during football season, you would more than likely find Chip at Grant Field or wherever Tech was playing its away game. He also followed other College teams to see how the players might measure up to his Yellow Jackets. On some Saturdays, he would attend one game in the morning, and then take a plane to get to another night game in a different city. He was the definition of a football fan.

He derived great joy from doing projects for Tech with his fellow alumni. In 1953 he helped with a new building on campus which was called the T Club Building, and he furnished all of the rooms for the club. Chip did many projects to help students feel more welcomed on the Tech campus, and it would be impossible to actually know the total number of students that benefited from his financial assistance.

After World War II, when Chip was spending a great deal of time in Japan, he made many friends which he kept for the rest of his life. He stayed in touch with their families, and supplied the tuition for several Japanese boys to attend and graduate from Georgia Tech.

During the 1940's, Ralph McGill wrote a column about a wartime football game at Georgia

Tech. McGill had been working in his office, and decided to walk over and catch some of the game. He really loved watching Bill Alexander coach, and he called him 'the old man'. McGill said that win or lose, you could always see an interesting game if 'the old man' was coaching the Yellow Jackets.

McGill noted that it was a different atmosphere at Grant Field, all during the war years, with young men in uniform filling the stands. He observed that these soldiers were just boys about to go overseas, and that everything seem changed in this 'war season' for many reasons.

After a while of sitting in the bleachers, McGill wandered up to the press box, and there was his friend Chip Robert hidden in the back of one of the boxes. He first sat with Chip but could hardly stand how Chip jabbed him with his elbows. Chip squirmed and twisted with every play and could not sit still for one moment. Before long, McGill made an excuse to leave and went to another press box. He sat down next to a colleague who told him he had moved away from Chip for the same reason.

Until 1971, Chip made many trips to Africa, one of his and Evie's favorite destinations. Evie was very involved with wildlife conservation, and she helped out at the zoos in Atlanta and Washington. They really enjoyed their African adventures together over the years. Also, Chip owned the Coca Cola bottling plant in Nairobi, and he and his family frequented various regions of Kenya whenever they traveled to that part of the world. Chip always had his polaroid camera. Once, he was traveling in a very remote region of Africa and visiting a local tribe which was very primitive. When he took a picture of the chieftain, the camera immediately ejected the fully-developed image, and the tribe went wild. They thought the polaroid was some kind of evil spirit and they grabbed the camera away from Chip and destroyed it. Birney said they felt their lives could really be in danger, but it all turned out OK. Chip really took that camera everywhere he went.

Kenya was a very interesting country, and Nairobi was a very sophisticated capital city. Not far from here, there was a fabulous resort called Treetops, where guests could actually spend the night in charming cottages built up in the trees. All kinds of wildlife would roam about right under these trees, and it was a perfect way to see the animals up close without being in danger. On one of their visits Queen Elizabeth and Prince Phillip were also there. It was 1952, and they were all in the hotel at the moment when a line of limousines pulled up to whisk the then Princess Elizabeth away because her father, King George VI, had just died, leaving her to become 'The Crown' at age twenty-six. She was coronated Queen Elizabeth II on June 7, 1953. And coincidentally, Chip's son and grandson, Chip, attended the coronation that summer.

Chip was also very familiar with Southeast Asia, and had been going there for many years. He took one trip in 1957 with his daughter, Birney and his old friend, Price Gilbert, which turned out to be the last trip to Saigon. This is how the story was told by Birney:

The three of us had been on a tour of the Angkor Wat ruins in Cambodia, and we had returned to our hotel in Saigon and had retired for the evening. Sometime in the middle of the night, the hotel manager woke us up and told us that we must evacuate immediately. We were told to leave in the dark, and not to wait until daybreak. And that Vietnam had already begun to close all the borders.

Panic ensued since certain papers had to be signed before they could leave the country, and it was too early for the embassy or diplomatic offices to be open for business. Fortunately, Birney spoke some French and so she and Chip and Price went to the residence of a diplomatic consul, and waited outside his door until someone eventually allowed them entrance. The diplomat eventually stamped their passports and put their papers in order. From there, they literally ran to the train station, but just barely missed the last train. There were no cars for hire, but Chip managed to pay an elderly farmer to drive them in his truck to try and catch a train to take them across the border. Well, it so happened that Price had bought a very large, live, white duck, which he was lugging along with him all the while. Price was also constantly puffing on his cigars.

The rickety old truck was cramped and uncomfortable and they had been riding for many hours. Finally, when they stopped in a rice paddy late in the night, they all got out to stretch their legs and Chip told Price that if he did not get rid of that duck and those smelly cigars, that he was going to leave him in the rice paddy field. So they found a farmer who offered to take the duck and they did finally make it to the train only seconds before it departed. After they got settled on the train, they were trying to find some food since it had been nearly a day since they had eaten. Birney had found some chocolate covered ants and Chip had purchased a big package of cheese. He and Price were starving but as they eagerly unwrapped the generous chunk of cheese, hundreds of maggots swarmed from the paper and onto their laps. Birney said they stayed hungry until they reached their destination.

1963 was a banner year for Chip and for Georgia Tech. Chip was born in 1887 and that was the same year that Tech really got started. Chip always said that he and Tech were the same age. The year 1963 marked the 75th Anniversary for both.

Chip had decided that he wanted to give some special gift to his alma mater, and so he presented the school with a check for $75,000 for unrestricted use for the school. This was the largest gift of unrestricted funds that had ever been received at that time.

The October, 1963 *Ramblin' Wreck* reported, in part:

Now the history of Georgia Tech is full of Chip Robert's contributions to his alma mater. And measured against his part in starting the co-operative division, or convincing the athletic board that the late W.A. Alexander deserved a shot at the head coaching job here back in 1920, this gift might seem insignificant. But the people here on the campus don't buy this line of thought. To us, this is a starting point—an unselfish gesture by the 1908 graduate who as much as any other alumnus has helped shape the face of today's Georgia Tech. As his letter points out, he is attempting to influence other alumni to insure the future growth of Georgia Tech.

Below is the text of this letter from Chip Robert which accompanied his donation check. In his message to President Harrison, Chip speaks of the great value which his alma mater has added to his life:

Dear President Harrison:

Inasmuch as Georgia Tech is now celebrating its 75th Anniversary, and, incidentally, my Class of 1908 its 55th Reunion, I cannot imagine a more propitious time to choose to make a gesture of my deep affection toward my beloved Alma Mater. Therefore, it is my privilege and pleasure at this time to tender to the Georgia Institute of Technology through the Georgia Tech Foundation, Inc., a 75th Anniversary Memorial Gift of seventy-five thousand dollars ($75,000,00) to aid you and your able associates in the future development of this fine institution, which has already made itself such a major part of our community, our state, and our nation in scientific and educational affairs.

Please pardon personal references but it was just sixty years ago this summer, shortly before my sixteenth birthday, that I took one of my life's most vital steps. While en route to Cornell University with hopes for a college engineering education, I stopped over in Atlanta to enter the Georgia School of Technology as a Sub-Apprentice to make up for my lack of high school opportunities. This school was then a young and struggling institution, but somehow it soon demonstrated to me in its own ambitious endeavors the very goals I myself aspired to. It is history now that I never left Georgia Tech for Cornell University, but instead I remained for six years to graduate in the Class of 1908 and added an extra post-graduate year in 1909.

My decision to remain at Georgia Tech has never caused me a single regret. To the contrary, it has brought me great happiness and memories. I have lived to love and honor this fine institution more and more as the years have passed. I have lived to see Georgia Tech rise to great heights, developing most enviable and honorable traditions as it steered along in its course, always aspiring and aiming at the very best in education our nation could produce.

Further, it has been my good fortune to remain close by in Atlanta after my graduation. Therefore, I have been able to watch at close range as Georgia Tech grew to its present status. Along with many others of our loyal alumni and friends, I have reveled in its reflected glory and accomplishments. Needless to say, all of this has meant a great deal to me in my life, and I feel most happy that I can now express in a somewhat more substantial way my deep love and gratitude by making this particular gift to Tech on its 75th Anniversary.

I am asking our Georgia Tech Foundation, through its Officers and Directors, to accept this Memorial Gift so that they along with you can see that it is used in the ways that will mean most to Georgia Tech and my native State and to add to the institution's ability to further carry on its fine aspirations and traditions for which all of us as alumni and friends are so justly proud.

The present outstanding educational and research program which our Governor and his Ad-

Georgia Tech 50th Reunion

ministration are so ably and strongly endorsing is the kind of program to make our college more and more the valuable asset so needed in our State and which I so strongly endorse and support.

It is my hope that this personal gift along with other similar gifts I am sure will follow may give further impetus to such valuable programs in helping make available to our young people of the future who might choose a career at Georgia Tech the very best in education and environment toward successful careers. Also I hope these same young people will find this success by staying and prospering right here in our own wonderful State and Southland. There exist no greater opportunities anywhere than are afforded right here at home. [Signed, with highest esteem to President Harrison, Chip Robert]

There is an interesting and amusing story that happened during this same year. In 1963, some student pranksters at Georgia Tech climbed to the roof of the power plant on campus and took the steam whistle. This venerable old whistle had been sounding off on the hour every day from 7 a.m. until 5 p.m for 75 years and it signaled the change of classes at Tech.

Chip's Atlanta home for many years was the Biltmore Hotel near the campus, and he had come to rely on this old whistle as his morning alarm clock and suddenly there was no whistle.

It did not take long for Chip to set about to replace 'his personal alarm clock'. Chip located a replacement whistle and had it delivered to Georgia Tech. Here is a part of his letter to Dean George Griffin on November 22, 1963:

This whistle came off one of the old famous Southern Railroad locomotives that pulled the Crescent Limited—New York to New Orleans Limited, back when it was known as "old #37 and #38" on the run between Washington and Atlanta. This was about the same time as our friend, Bill Brosnan was a student at Georgia Tech…long before he could have dreamed that one day he would become the President of Southern Railway Company.

Then Chip requested that the new whistle which had been checked out and cleaned by the Railroad employees, should be christen the 'Bill Brosnan Big Ben', and that's how Tech got its whistle back.

The year 1965 brought Chip a unique honor in the form of the Eloy Alfaro Grand Cross and diploma of the Foundation of the Republic of Panama. This ceremony was held in New York City on April 14, 1965 to honor Chip's life of outstanding humanitarian service. Senator Herman Talmadge made a speech in Congress about Chip and his honor, and noted that six former US Presidents, several state Governors, and other luminaries had also been honored with the Alfaro Cross.

The following story is about Coach Bobby Dodd and illustrates a heartfelt relationship between Chip Robert and the coach, and their love of Georgia Tech and of the game of football.

It is the year 1975 and Georgia Tech is hosting a retirement dinner for coach Bobby Dodd who has been coaching Tech football for 40 years. The school is preparing for him a scrapbook which is filled with clippings, pictures, and letters from all sorts of alumni and notable figures from Coach Dodd's past. The dinner is set for October 17, and many at Tech have been writing and calling Chip's office to remind him to write a letter to coach Dodd.

Although Chip has not responded, employees at the Athletic Association and the Tech Foundation continue to try and reach him, and they learn that Chip is very ill, In fact he would live only seven more months—he died June 9, 1976 in his 88th year. However, on October 14, 1975 Chip does deliver his letter for the scrapbook, and it is beautiful in every sense of the word. It is quoted, almost in its entirety below:

> *Dear Bobby,*
>
> *It is with the greatest memories and everlasting devotion that I salute you. Neither you nor I can and will ever forget the first meeting that we had in my Atlanta office late in the year 1930 ....For at least a year, as Chair of the Georgia Tech Athletic Board,....I had been trying to determine, as best I could, where we should go to secure an outstanding backfield coach for old coach Alex (William Alexander was Tech's head football coach)...We would want him to become a prominent citizen of Atlanta and the State of Georgia so that his football career at Georgia Tech in the years to come, would be an honor and credit to our institution.*
>
> *I asked you about your ambitions in life and the career you hoped to follow, and I still emphasized that we did not want just an ordinary football coach, and even further we wanted you to tie yourself to our city and our community...and so we shook hands and struck a deal.*
>
> *Your faculty at the University of Tennessee was greatly impressed by our discussion....but shocked to lose you from that school...I made sure, talking with your faculty, that you would have your proper credits to graduate, and we worked it out with the University of Tennessee (that your remaining courses could be taken here at Georgia Tech).*
>
> *This hour, Bobby, was a great time of destiny for both you and Georgia Tech, and was one of the happiest moments of my life....You have been Georgia Tech's most prominent coach, athletic director, faculty representative, and alumnus since that day. The great honor that you have brought to yourself, you have endowed to Georgia Tech and every other alumnus or friend of Georgia Tech, certainly including me, lives in great appreciation of what you have given to our beloved Alma Mater. I have many times been urged to write the complete story of your coming to our institution but it would take volumes for me to ever attempt such a story...*
>
> *It is my great pleasure and everlasting appreciation that I thank you from the bottom of my heart how completely you have fulfilled a great deal more than one hundred per cent what you had decided that day when you joined hands with us....*
>
> *Nearing my 90th year, it is my hope and prayer that you will enjoy good health and happiness for many more years to come. Needless to say, this all comes from the bottom of my heart and an unmatched experience in my life.*
>
>
>
> *Ever faithfully yours with great affection,*
> *Chip*
>
>

For sure, Chip Robert did deliver quite a letter.

During his life, Chip granted dozens of interviews to Georgia Tech reporters, and in 1964, *The Georgia Tech Engineer Magazine* interviewed him for an article entitled, 'The Engineer in Perspective', The Tech reporter asked Chip for his views concerning the importance of a liberal arts education to all students, and more especially to engineers.

Chip offered these viewpoints as a part of the interview:

> *The original concept for the education of an engineer, encompassed the idea that he should be prepared to serve society more fully, by having a sufficient grounding in the humanities and this leads to a well rounded life…and The humanities and social sciences are, in a very serious sense, practical and useful.…In order to meet his growing responsibilities and to realize his capabilities as a human being, as well as to lead a more enjoyable life, the engineer needs both professional competence and a broad understanding of himself and of the world. He needs depth and flexibility, and a capacity for growth. Of course, it goes without saying that a major part of anyone's being broadened is up to himself.*

Chip and Evie out West in Wyoming, 1940's

CHAPTER TEN

Every Life has an Ending

*To sleep I give my powers away; my will is bondsman to the dark; I sit
within a helmless bark, and with my heart, I muse and say; Oh heart,
how fares it with thee now, that thou should fail from thy desire?
Who scarcely darest to inquire, 'what is it that makes me beat so low?'
Something it is which thou hast lost, some pleasure from thine early years.
Break the deep vase of chilling tears, that grief hath shaken into frost!
Such clouds of nameless troubles cross, all night below the darkened eyes; With
morning wakes the will and cries, thou shalt not be the fool of loss.*

Alfred, Lord Tennyson (from In Memoriam)

As the years passed by, Chip stayed the course of his 'purpose-driven' life. He continued on with his vision for his firm and increased his involvement with his alma mater. His life was rich with friends and family, but he had suffered terrible losses during his final years. Many of his cherished friends had passed away; he had endured the tragic death of his only son in 1962; and, a decade later, his beloved Evie, who was twenty years his junior, succumbed to her desperate five-year battle with kidney disease. After this blow in 1972, Chip was never the same. The photographs of him during his last few years reveal a stricken countenance, and his gaze seems to be always toward some faraway place.

But he stayed active and enjoyed his work to aid Georgia Tech in any way within his power. During the turbulent civil rights era of the 60s, Chip had a standing weekly meeting with the City Fathers, elected officials, and business leaders to confer about ways in which they could ensure that desegregation in Atlanta would be successfully accomplished completely and peaceably. Chip had been, for decades, one of the most ardent supporters of Morehouse and Spellman Colleges in Atlanta. He was a most generous financial supporter of both institutions and helped cause the Board of Regents to increase these schools' share of Georgia State funding.

Chip continued to be an official delegate to every National Democratic Convention. He was scheduled to be there in New York for the 1976 convention, but died on the very day in which Georgia's native son, Jimmy Carter was nominated. It was a salute to Chip's memory, that the convention hall paused for a moment of silence on that day when it was announced that Chip had passed away.

He continued to travel far and wide until a few months before his death and he loved to visit his daughter Louisa at Sea Island. Georgia and his daughter Birney, at Warrenton, Virginia. Chip always enjoyed visits with his grandchildren and their families. He continued to get together with his Atlanta friends and to attend every Georgia Tech football game and most of the baseball home games, and he loved celebrating birthdays and holidays.

It is appropriate to note here, that his favorite time of the year was Christmas, and this holiday he celebrated with great delight and even greater generosity.

Since 1917, when he started his own firm Chip began a tradition of sending Christmas treats to all his friends, family, employees and associates. His very first gifts were boxes of apples, and even back then, he carefully saved each and every note of thanks that he ever received.

Soon, Chip was sending fresh pecans from Lanett, Alabama. He also began sending fresh country sausage and cured hams from South Georgia. In a few years, he had added fresh Georgia salted pecan halves, Sorgham syrup from Rabun Gap, fresh peach preserves and Mae West Turkeys from Callaway Gardens. No one ever loved southern food more than Chip. He sent different delicacies to different friends and some received more than one type of gift.

He often mentioned in his letters, of his great passion for old fashioned southern cooking and of how he would dream of his favorite meal; turnip greens with 'pot likker', ham or fried chicken, corn bread and for dessert, sweet potato custard pie.

The things that are remarkable about this seemingly ordinary gift-giving tradition are several. For one thing, he never missed a season of Christmas giving during all those many years. The one time that was different happened during World War II in 1942. Chip did not want to clog up the postal system, he said, when the soldiers would be wanting packages from home, so he wrote a Christmas note asking each friend to buy War Bonds instead of giving gifts, and to pray for peace. Surprisingly, he received more thank you notes on that Christmas than any past year—everyone thought this was a grand idea.

Another striking thing is that for every year since the 1920s, Chip's secretary (first, Mrs. Mize until her death in 1948 and then Miss Lewis until Chip died) kept a typed annual Christmas gift recipient list in separate files, each with its own list of names and addresses and each file contained every thank you note he received. These Christmas gift recipient lists were many dozens of pages long every year.

The other remarkable thing is that the number kept growing and growing up until the year he died. By 1975, the number of turkeys sent out each year was 380; country hams—200; sausage 300 orders; and the boxes of salted pecans numbered almost a thousand. And note that this was his annual list, not his total for all lists.

Once, when he learned that a few of his friends had used the salted pecans for 'Christmas baking', he wrote a memo to Miss Lewis to change their gift to another food. He was horrified that such a delicacy as salted pecan halves should be squandered on 'baked goods' when he believed they should be savored like a fine wine, a small bite at a time to get the full flavor. He was definitely a southern cuisine expert. And in addition to these special foods, his files are replete with order forms for Della Robbia wreaths, fruitcakes and other holiday treats. Imagine all of these files, steadily growing each year for nearly sixty years, Chip's record of gratitude to his friends.

There is a somewhat saddening footnote to this. A letter fell from a box while we were unloading some containers of Chip's papers from storage. This letter had never been opened and had been written to him in 1976. It was sent by the manager of the Mayflower Hotel to his apartment in Washington (Suites 777, 778, and 779), and in it, the manager was asking about Mr. Robert's health and saying that no one at the Mayflower had seen him for several months, and everyone was wondering where he was. The letter went on to say that they urgently needed Mr. Robert's attention to a problem. It seemed that the freezers in the Mayflower kitchens were filled with Mr. Robert's turkeys and that the kitchen was in dire need of the space.

These were turkeys which Chip had sent from Callaway Gardens as Christmas presents, but for some reason or another, could not be delivered. So the turkeys were returned to the Mayflower. The manager pleaded, 'Please, Sir, could you advise us immediately as to what we should do with your property. We fear that some of the parcels are long since spoiled, and we really must have the space.'

There is one more turkey tale that begs to be told. Chip and his friends were always playing practical jokes on one another. There was constantly some hilarious happening afoot among these guys, each trying to out-prank the other.

One Christmas, Chip enclosed a special turkey dressing recipe in a few of the turkeys which were going to his good but unsuspecting pals. Chip's note said that this recipe was an old southern favorite for stuffing with a surprising flavor. The printed recipe was the prank. It listed normal ingredients used to prepare cornbread stuffing, but also included 'One heaping cup of uncooked popcorn'.

Chip had only to wait until Christmas Day for the telephone calls to start coming in. One friend on the west coast was having their turkey cooked in an outdoor kitchen. His friend heard a loud noise, and lo and behold, the turkey had blown out of the stove and through the screen door. Another friend in New York called to say that their turkey had exploded in the oven and fell out onto the floor.

Chip laughed and laughed, and told all his distraught callers to just pick up the turkey and eat it, and that it would still be delicious. He did think that they would surely have known better than to put raw popcorn kernels into a turkey! Chip really loved that prank.

This seemingly disconnected tale of turkeys, does have a great significance and deep meaning. It was Chip's true and tangible sign of his abiding love and gratitude for his fellow man. He would not miss this festive occasion to express his thanks to all who had given him assistance, and pleasure during the past year.

Often, in his later years, Chip wrote poignant letters to his friends thanking them for all the years of friendship. He would say how he could just close his eyes and dream of all the memories of their adventures and wonderful trips together. He would say that he considered the friendships that he had made during his whole life to be his endowment which could never be taken away. He said he would carry the memories in his heart forever.

He felt this in particular for the hundreds of life long associations he had formed through the years at Tech. Many times he had said that it was his belief that everything he had become, and all of his successes in business and in life, were due largely to his experiences at Georgia Tech. He was always quick to give credit to his alma mater, and forever devoted to her causes.

Shortly after Chip's death, The Board of Regents wrote to his daughters:

> *Mr. Chip has long been identified with civic endeavors. His service on the Board of Regents ...was marked by an unselfish devotion to the highest ideals, principles and purposes of higher education. His death will also leave a void in the ranks of the staunch friends and supporters of Georgia Tech. Certainly, no alumnus has ever been more loyal to his alma mater.... Chip Robert lived a long and productive life, and made significant and lasting contributions to the welfare of our State and Nation. In the hearts and minds of those who loved him, we know that time will bring a cherished memory in place of present sorrow.*

In the June 14, 1976 issue of the Congressional Record (S9171) Senator Hubert Humphrey addressed the members of the Senate as follows:

> *It was with deep sadness that I learned of the death of Lawrence Wood Robert, Jr. on June 9, in Atlanta, Georgia. The Nation has lost a distinguished citizen and a versatile public figure, and I have lost a good and dear friend.*
>
> *By the time that America was entering the age of specialization, Chip Robert had already succeeded at a number of careers. Athlete, scholar and gentleman, Chip Robert was trained to be an engineer at his beloved Georgia Tech. But he became one of the principal architects of the New Deal. He must have known, however, that he would become an outstanding Democrat. Indeed, as early as 1930, he raised $27,000 in Georgia for Roosevelt's gubernatorial campaign in New York,—an event without parallel in its time, and probably never duplicated.*
>
> *From there, Chip Robert went on to become a close friend and confidant of FDR, and served as Assistant Secretary of the Treasury. He served with distinction as the Secretary of the National Democratic Party during the great days when Jim Farley was Chairman.*
>
> *Yet, for all his prominence, Chip Robert never lost his love for the South. As the head of Robert and Company, the noted engineering and architectural firm, he was a tireless advocate for his native region, and convinced many businesses to locate there. For that reason, among many others, I was both pleased and honored when he agreed to manage my campaign in Georgia in 1968.*

In all the years that I knew him, Chip Robert was always a man of much wisdom and unfailing charm. I am proud to have had him as a fellow Democrat and a personal friend, and I am sure that the State of Georgia and the Nation as a whole will miss him greatly.

On June 11, 1976, Senator Herman Talmadge spoke about the life of Chip Robert on the floor of the Senate, and this tribute was recorded in the Congressional Record (S9094):

One of Georgia's most outstanding citizens and a great American, Mr. Lawrence Wood "Chip" Robert, Jr. died on Wednesday in Atlanta. I join the people of Georgia and his many friends and loved ones throughout the United States in mourning the passing of this fine man....It is not often that there is produced a man of the caliber of Chip Robert, whose leadership, service, and gentlemanly qualities were an inspiration to all with whom he came in contact in his personal, professional and business life.

It may be that no other political figure who never ran for any elected office at all, has ever received such praise from elected officials.

The National newspapers all reported the death of Chip Robert and there were many stories about his life. The *Atlanta Constitution* reported on June 10, 1976 in part:

Down through the years, Robert combined his business genius with a flair for national politics and he was a charmer of the most sophisticated circles of Washington, New York and Palm Beach.

One paper, in speaking of his accomplishments, said that the death of Chip Robert had left a hole in the heart of Georgia Tech which would be impossible to fill.

James A. Farley, Chairman of the DNC during the glory years, and closest friend of Chip, died just two hours after hearing of the death of Chip. They were both 88 years old. A reporter called Jim Farley before he died to get his reaction to Chip's death. Farley said that he loved Chip like a brother and that they had remained close during all the years. Farley said one of the highlights of his life had been to meet Chip back in April for a reunion at Warm Springs Georgia which included those men who had been responsible for the preservation of Roosevelt's Little White House and the Foundation there in Warm Springs.

Charlie Roberts wrote a Eulogy about Chip on behalf of the *Georgia Tech Magazine*. In his article he said in part:

The heart of Chip Robert stopped beating on June 9, 1976....But this one of Georgia Tech's greatest alumni did not die. He keeps right on living in the folklore of his beloved school and in the grateful hearts of Tech men everywhere...(This is a story of) a man and his devotion to the school that gave him his chance in life, a wonderkind—great athlete who was the only Georgia Tech Sports figure ever to earn 15 athletic letters. (He was) a scholar, a member of the Uni-

versity System Board of Regents, the Tech Board of Trustees for 24 years, and a member of the Tech Athletic Board constantly down through the years. He was a volunteer coach in football and baseball and a tutor of Calculus for the student athletes. He was a recruiter of athletes and coaches for his alma mater and he was a super fund raiser. He was the most influential alumnus of his time and he often said 'Anything that Tech needs and wants, I think Tech should have it.'

Thus it was, that after 88 years upon this Earth. The life of Lawrence Wood Robert, Jr. had its ending. But his memory is with us still to remind us of the value of his remarkable life and legacy.

One friend said that:

To remember Chip was to invoke happy memories of great companionship, of successes and of failures, and all of the adventures colored by his charm and his joyful nature.

Any memory of Chip Robert is flavored by his winning smile, his jovial wit, and his hilarious stories and jokes, which he could spin out at a moment's notice. Those who knew him said that his laughter could fill a room. He recounted tales of his world travels, of long ago Georgia Tech football and baseball triumphs and of his beloved South and its traditions which he cherished. Especially, he was forever telling about Georgia Tech and what she had meant to him for all the years of his life. Chip's enduring love for and abiding faith in Georgia Tech was the constant of his whole life and Georgia Tech was his bedrock. Chip always gave his alma mater full credit and gratitude for any and all successes he might have made in his personal or professional life.

Chip possessed a brilliant mind, a relentless striving for accomplishment, a sharp sense of intuition, and he had the gift of optimism. He had a sixth sense for creating long-range plans and strategies, which served him well in his professional life.

Chip had an unflagging curiosity about everything, and he was addicted to travel. He was constantly on the go, whether by ship, train or plane and he was said to have logged more miles just from Atlanta to Washington, DC than any Congressman or Senator from any state had ever traveled in total.

It seemed the spirit of youth was always with him, and his delight in living and his joyful temperament were contagious.

Of all the many achievements of his extraordinary life, his greatest achievement may have been the development of his own personality. Chip Robert's life was, in fact, a beautiful work of art.

No man knew better than Chip of the temporary nature of worldly fame and fortune. And he certainly never relied on either of these conditions. He never claimed to be perfect, nor did he expect perfection in his friends. He knew that everyone was flawed, and he was quick to come to the aid of a friend in need.

Chip believed that it was not the great victories or defeats which mark our lives, but rather that we are measured by the manner in which we face up to adversity and tragedy. Likewise, Chip believed the true test of character was the way in which one dealt with great failure or success. Chip said it was not so much what happens to us, but how we respond to our situations that really shows our character.

It is clear that, for Chip, there was no separating his business from his personal life. His work was his delight and his pleasure, and he made business actually fun. His style was always to work behind the scenes, seldom, if ever claiming any credit for the results. It was unimportant to him who got the credit. He seemed so comfortable in his own skin and so self confident that he simply had no need for ratification or praise. He was too busy to take time for affirmation. Once he had accomplished the thing he had set out to do, he was on to the next project just because that was his nature.

So, here at the end of this story, we are searching for the answer to some questions. What was the measure of the life of Chip Robert, and what legacy does he leave for us?

Now that he has been gone for nearly a half century, what light shines from his example for us to follow? What are the values that he held dear? And how did one self-made man manage to do so much good in one lifetime? What really is the measure of his life?

Chip Robert certainly lived his life at a full gallop. His aspirations were never ending. He felt that every worthy cause was his cause, that civic duty was the privilege of every citizen, and that kindness was a responsibility.

He was a shining example of the timeless virtues by which he lived: loyalty without question; service to his neighbor; generosity in all things; integrity without compromise; excellence in his profession; devotion to his nation; sacrifice so that his countrymen could have a better life; and constant gratitude. He was, in every sense, a patriot.

For Chip, these were the values that guided him through his entire life. They are values as relevant today as they have ever been. They are values necessary in a modern world.

If there was a job Chip thought should be done, then no assignment was too hard, no journey was too long, and no sacrifice was too great. He did his very best, no matter what the cost, to see that the job was done, and done well.

At every time, in every age, and especially now, every one of us is searching for a hero.

It has been said that a hero is not a person who does one particular great or noble thing at one particular time. Rather it can be said that a true hero is a person who inspires others by the example of his own way of life. A hero leads by many small examples of courage and kindness which, in turn, encourage many ordinary people to do extraordinary things. A hero gives inspiration to every generation, to lead their own courageous lives in service to others.

The life of Lawrence Wood Robert, Jr. was truly the Life of a Hero.

ACKNOWLEDGEMENTS

THIS PROJECT HAS been a unique experience, and I have been helped by many friends. Learning something of the life and times of The Honorable Lawrence Wood 'Chip' Robert Jr. has been a thrilling journey.

I want to express my heartfelt gratitude for the life of the Late Chip Robert, Jr. He has inspired me with his integrity, cheered me with jovial charm, and disarmed me with his easy grace. He has uplifted me with his optimism and humbled me with his patriotism. Chip Robert was a loyal American, a devoted friend, a helpmate to his family and a generous alumnus of Georgia Tech, the place he held so dear. He aided and comforted his fellow citizens in countless acts of kindness for his entire life. Thank you Chip Robert, Jr. for teaching me the true meaning of gratitude, devotion and loyalty.

I thank The Stuart A. Rose Manuscript Archives & Rare Book Library at Emory University for acquiring the entire collection of the papers and materials of the late Lawrence Wood 'Chip' Robert Jr., and in so doing, affirming the importance of his life and accomplishments. And in particular, I wish to thank Rosemary Magee and Randy Gue for their tireless efforts in bringing this gift home to my alma mater. These professionals are a part of the important work going on every day campus wide, that makes Emory University one of the finest institutions anywhere in the world.

The Rose Library has as its mission, the connecting of stories of human experience; the promotion of access and learning; and the offering of opportunities for dialogue for all wise hearts who seek knowledge. It also has as its mission, the preservation of distinctive collections; the fostering of original research, the bridging of content and context, and the engagement of diverse communities through innovative outreach, programming, and exhibitions.

For the design and production of this book, I shall be evermore grateful to my new best friends at Gorham Printing company in Centralia, Washington.

I am always grateful for my daughters, and especially now, want to thank Birney Robert and Georgia Robert Parmelee for the time and patience they have spent helping with the editing,

Acknowledgements

Above: Four Robert generations from left to right: LWR Sr. (The Captain), LWR IV, LWR III and LWR, Jr. Below: A later photo of the four generations from left to right: LWR III, The Captain, LWR, Jr. Front: LWR IV

and various software mishaps. Sorry for all those late night calls.

With great love and gratitude to Aunt Birney, the only surviving child of our Hero, who has been the steward of his papers for all of these years. She has kept them safe and intact and in good condition for more than forty two years, and we are grateful that she is now sharing them with all of us. If she had not taken the time, energy and expense to preserve her father's papers, no one now or in the future would ever have the opportunity to discover his legacy. Thanks Aunt Birney!

I appreciate each and every person, dead or alive, whom I have referenced or quoted in this book. I have tried to give proper credit, and if I have fallen short in that regard, I ask for your forgiveness. Any errors or omissions were unintentional and accidental and I am truly sorry.

Last but not least, I give my heartfelt thanks to my husband, Lawrence Wood 'Chip' Robert, IV, the grandson of Lawrence Wood 'Chip' Robert, Jr. My Chip has given me his endless support and patience during every step of this endeavor, and when the work became bogged down, he urged me to carry on and not to give up. Many were the evenings he and I spent in front of the fire in fall and winter, and on the porch in the spring and summer sifting through hundreds of boxes and thousands of pieces of paper as we put the files in chronological order. And it is also to him that this book is happily dedicated.

SOURCES CONSULTED

Brittain, M.L. *The Story of Georgia Tech*. Chapel Hill. The University of North Carolina Press. 1948

Bruner, Robert F. (and Sean D. Carr) *The Panic of 1907*. Hoboken. John A. Wilely & Sons, Inc. 2007.

Burns, James M. *Roosevelt: The Soldier of Freedom*. New York. Harcourt, Brace Jovanovich, Inc.1970

Clay, Lucius D. *Decision in Germany*. New York. Doubleday Company, Inc. 1950.

Dodd, Robert. *Bobby Dodd on Football*. New York. The Strode Publishers. 1954.

Grady, Henry. *The New South*. Savannah. The Beehive Press. 1971.

Griffin, George. *Griffin, You are a Great Disappointment to Me*. Atlanta. The Georgia Tech National Alumni Association. 1971.

Hamilton, Nigel. *The Mantel of Command; FDR at War*. New York. Houghton Mifflin Harcourt Publishing Company. 2014.

Hill, Dean. *Football Through the Years*. New York. Gridiron Publishing Company. 1940.

International Library of Technology. Scranton. International Textbook Company. 1922.

Little, Tom. *The Wearers of the T*. Montgomery. L&M Corporation. 1966.

Martin, Harold. *William Berry Hartsfield, Mayor of Atlanta*. Athens. The University of Georgia Press. 1975.

McCullough, David. *Truman.* New York, Simon & Shuster. 1992.

McGill, Ralph E. *Ralph Emerson McGill.* Atlanta. Mary Lynn McGill. 1970.

McGill, Ralph. *The South and the Southerner.* Boston. Little Brown & Company. 1959

Pearl Harbor Day Pamphlet. Public Information Office. Honolulu. Commander in Chief, Pacific & US Fleet. 1951.

Phillips, Capt. C. A. *The Miracle of War.* Cherry Point. Third Marine Aircraft Wing. 1942.

Rice, Grantland (and O.B. Keeler). *The Bobby Jones Story.* Atlanta. Tupper & Love. 1953.

Russell, James M. *Atlanta 1847–1890.* Baton Rouge, Louisiana State University Press. 1988.

Stinnett, Ronald. *Democrats, Dinners & Dollars.* Des moines, Iowa State University Press. 1967.

Thomy, Al. *The Ramblin' Wreck, A Story of Georgia Tech Football.* The Strode Publishers. Huntsville. 1973.

Twain, Mark. *The Innocents Abroad.* San Francisco, 1869.

Wallace, Robert B. *Dress Her In White and Gold.* Atlanta. The Georgia Tech Foundation, Inc., 1963.

Georgia Tech football dinner 1942, Pres. Brittain, Bobby Dodd, Chip, Mayor Harsfield, etc.

Evie with young tiger

Guests at the Jackson Day $100 per plate dinner held at the Mayflower Hotel on Jan. 7th, 1939. The President may be seen at the center of the main table.

Mrs. Eleanor Roosevelt giving a speech at the Democratic National Convention of 1940. Chip at left with folded arms.

**Chip always hosted the annual Navy League dinner.
Shown here with Carl Vinson and Admiral McDowal, 1965.**

Chip (second from left) at Coca Cola gathering, Atlanta.

Cabinet Council, 1933

The "Gang of Six" on the campaign trail, 1936

Atlanta Candler Field Airport inaugural flight, 1932. American Airways, Atlanta to Houston
(Louisa Robert Christens)

Chip Robert, Secretary of the Democratic National Committee, with Mrs. Barkley.

Evie and Chip

Chip resting at Cottage #12, Sea Island.

Chip's staff party on the occasion of his retirement from the DNC in 1940. Note the fake campaign buttons, "We don't want Chip either."

Chip at his retirement dinner looking through his scrapbook.

Chip enjoying a good laugh with Vice President Garner and President Roosevelt.

President Franklin Delano Roosevelt in his first term.

ROBERT AND COMPANY
ARCHITECTS & ENGINEERS
FOR
TEXTILE MILLS AND INDUSTRIAL PLANTS
ATLANTA

April 6, 1921.

Mr. N. I. Hirsch,
Columbus, Ga.

My dear Fellow Alumnus:

Remember, in the old days when the Tech Football Team was the official doormat for the S.I.A.A. before Jack Heisman took hold of it, and then Alec, and made it the Golden Tornado, feared and respected from the Gulf to Maine?

Remember, didn't you pull all the harder for the poor little old "Yellow Jackets" in those days, when they took their beating like the grand little heroes they were--and kept on coming back for more? Honest, now--- wasn't the Tech spirit then, isn't the Tech spirit NOW, the spirit that never quits fighting?

Remember, Leonard Wood -- if you're an old-timer, then Lobster Brown--, then "Twenty Percent" Davis,-- and on down to Everett Strupper, Buck Flowers, and Bill Fincher -- you've pulled for them all, winning and losing. And when it looked like a losing, hopeless battle, they didn't dog it, and you didn't dog it.

But I don't need to ask you that, old man. I know what your spirit was. And it was the spirit of Tech. I know what your spirit is now -- it is the spirit of Tech today.

All right, old man. Tech is in another battle today; the GREATEST and GRAVEST of her history. And it's the boosters that can put it over, in this game. This is your chance to do something, beside pull your head off for the renowned Golden Tornado.

Now Georgia Tech is in a campaign for $5,000,000 that will make our old school a Greater Georgia Tech; the kind of a school that fits the Golden Tornado, no longer the official doormat, but the same as our football machine that every coach in the country respects. Up in New York, Georgians and Tech men have challenged us down in Georgia, with an offer of $1,000,000 if we'd put over the rest of it.

That fund means a Greater Georgia Tech -- a Georgia Tech that will take care of an enrollment of 5,000 students--a Georgia Tech that can hold up her head among the technical schools of the country and of the world as her Golden Tornado stands out before the nation.

Tech can't win this battle with a football squad --- though the Golden Tornado has done its part. But the Tech spirit CAN win this battle. A Greater Georgia Tech should, and must, be grounded on Tech Alumni, as it will live always in their hearts.

Do this, if you are in the State of Georgia:
Go at once, and I mean at once not next week, to your local chairman and offer any assistance and cooperation within your power. Remember that in 95% of the cases your chairman is not a Georgia Tech man, but a man who has become interested in your Tech, and is willing to give his time and ability to help her get on top. If he is willing to do this, what should you from Georgia Tech be willing to do. Get together with the other Tech men in your community and make yourselves known. Let the local people know you are there and proud of Tech and anxious for its success, and **determined to back her to the limit.**

I tell you, old man, no possible excuse will go. This is the one time we have got to show ourselves and do a man-size job, and do it now. If you put it off, and hope somehow this proposition goes through without your help, or that some more loyal fellow will carry your part; you will regret it the **longest day you live.**

You may be already planning for for your boy to come to Tech, think of it, think what it means after all. What about it, will you help? There's a card enclosed for you to send back at once and tell us you are right and then put it over.

Here's hoping we all get together for Tech as never **before.**

Sincerely,

Chip Robert

LWR/o